The Symphony Writers
Since Beethoven

From a photo by E. Bieber, Berlin.

FELIX WEINGARTNER.

THE

SYMPHONY WRITERS SINCE BEETHOVEN

FRANZ SCHUBERT   ANTON BRÜCKNER
ROBERT SCHUMANN   HECTOR BERLIOZ
HERMANN GÖTZ   FRANZ LISZT
JOHANNES BRAHMS   RICHARD STRAUSS
PETER TCHAIKOVSKY   GUSTAV MAHLER
FELIX MENDELSSOHN-BARTHOLDY
CHARLES CAMILLE SAINT-SAENS, Etc.

BY

FELIX WEINGARTNER

FROM THE GERMAN BY

ARTHUR BLES

With Notice of the Author's own No. 5 Symphony by
D. C. Parker added to this issue

With Twelve Portraits

GREENWOOD PRESS, PUBLISHERS
WESTPORT, CONNECTICUT

Originally published in 1925
by William Reeves Bookseller Ltd., London

First Greenwood Reprinting 1971

Library of Congress Catalogue Card Number 77-109878

SBN 8371-4369-1

Printed in the United States of America

PREFACE TO THE AUTHOR'S ORIGINAL EDITION.

THE necessity, which has arisen in the second year after the first appearance of this treatise, of publishing a new edition is, to me, a gratifying proof that the ideas contained in it have not fallen on barren ground, though nothing has been done towards their further propagation.

This second edition differs from the first, not only in its greater smoothness of style, but also in its greater accuracy, the suppression of unnecessary detail, and insertion of important names and facts which did not appear before. It will be impossible in reading this edition to make such a mistake as to think that I do not believe in a possibility of the development of the symphony, or that I am a prejudiced advocate of the cause of programme music versus the symphony; it is even difficult to see how such a deduction could be drawn from the previous edition. Another objection made to the original book was that I had dismissed as unworthy of notice the names of several prominent composers. In Paris especially, where my treatise has become known through the medium of Madame Chevillard's translation, was this reproach made against me. Although this time I have mentioned more names than before, still even now those of many deserving men are left out. The book is not a register or dictionary of living or dead composers, and so the exactness and amplitude of such a work must not be expected from it.

And, finally, in answer to the question which

has been asked me, as to why, after writing down such thoughts as I have expressed in my book, I have had the impertinence to write two symphonies* myself, and what intention I had in writing them, I may say that I had no fixed intention at all; I simply wrote my two symphonies because the ideas contained in them came into my head.

---

* This has now been increased to five (1924). The last, No. 5, was first performed by the Scottish Orchestra, in Edinburgh, on December 8, 1924. An account of the work will be found in the Appendix to this volume.

LIST OF PORTRAITS.

CHAPTER I.

IF you have ever travelled through a beautiful valley, at the end of which, standing
among lesser hills, is some overtowering peak,
did you not, some time during your passage,
pause in admiring contemplation of its snow-
capped summit, lighting the horizon afar off;
perhaps even envy the good fortune of him
who could climb it, to revel in the splendid
view stretching away towards infinity? Supposing at such a moment, someone had suddenly come to you and said seriously, "I wish
to mount higher than that peak, to reach the
azure vault of Heaven," it is clear that you
would have at once thought that you were

I

dealing with a being, to say the least, bold and fantastic. Many of us, instead of laughing at such a man, would feel a deep sadness at the sight of him.

So does a light feeling of melancholy creep over me, when, knowing the greatness of Beethoven, and being penetrated by the profound bearing of his creations, I think of the many composers, who, after him, have undertaken and still undertake to write symphonies. Considering the immeasurable abundance of thought and sentiment expressed by Beethoven in his music, such an attempt seems almost as absurd as to wish to climb higher than the summit of a mountain. True, the outward appearance of the work is often similar to that of Beethoven's symphonies, sometimes even greater, but in no case does the composer possess that greatness of soul and profundity which were peculiar to Beethoven and enabled him to express all the grades of sentiment,

2

between the most tender love and the most violent passion, the frankest humour and metaphysical mysticism.

R. Wagner, not only the greatest artist, but also the greatest art-critic of the recent past, does not spare his sarcasm in regard to the post-Beethoven symphonists. He is astonished that composers have only seen the form of the master's creations, and have with an easy mind continued to write symphonies, ignorant of the fact that the last has already been written— that Ninth Symphony which he signals as the highest possible production of absolute music, as the direct transition, towards the work formed by the conjunction of all the arts, which delivers us from all uncertainty in the matter of artistic creation. According to his idea, the right of composing symphonies is abolished by this work.

Thus, to a certain extent, Wagner treats the Ninth Symphony as a forerunner of his own

3

life's work, and characterises Beethoven's greatest musical poem as a reformation such as he himself would have made.

I may as well state now, at the beginning of this treatise, that on this point I do not agree with Wagner's theory, as set forth in his "Opera and Drama." A nature such as his, endowed with incredible energy, which essayed to, and actually did, attain the height of its ambition, very naturally is inclined to regard all work not its own production in the light of simple ancestor, so to speak, thereby stultifying itself to some extent, in a way in which other great geniuses, not so revolutionary, such as Goethe, were not affected. We ask ourselves, What can one express in a form strictly bound by its own laws, of which the connection of the separate movements, the modulations, even, are all prescribed by laws almost immovable?

Is it possible to use this form again when one master has filled it with thoughts so vast

4

that it proved too small to contain them?
After expressing by it all the prodigious ideas
it could hold, he broke it as though he felt
it to be a chain, as in the last movement of the
Ninth Symphony, and several of his last sonatas and quartets.

Furthermore, we ask ourselves, If, instead
of yielding to an artistic impulse, composers
do not sometimes accomplish what is simply
a material work when, picking up, as it were,
the scattered débris of the form which burst
under the vast weight of Beethoven's thoughts,
they try to put it together as one whole, and
then to cork up the fissures. Of those who
thoughtlessly have dared to do this I ask,
"Have you really understood the greatness of
Beethoven?" One will answer to this that
Beethoven did not for ever renounce the habi-
tual form, and consequently one must not give
to this temporary abandonment the value of a
conclusive principle.

5

To the free Sonata (Op. 101), succeeds the monumental Sonata (Op. 106), with its four gigantic movements in perfect form. This work in its turn is followed by others again written freely, those in E major and A flat major. Then comes the last in C minor (Op. 111). Its finale, it is true, has not the precipitous rush common to the sonata, but apart from that, it is so perfect in form, that Von Bülow rightly hails it as a standing model of its species. The two Quartets in B flat major and C sharp minor, which are not in the usual form, come between those in E flat major and A minor, which do not differ in the slightest from the form of the preceding quartets. At any rate, it is clear that Beethoven never quitted the established form except when the plan of his whole work obliged him; that he did not consider it as abandoned or maintained because he left it and returned to it in a few isolated cases.

6

After duly considering all these examples, one has the right to presume, without affirming it, that Beethoven, had he lived longer, would, perhaps, after the Ninth Symphony, have written another in the old form (although Wagner's hypothesis of the "last symphony" has not generally engendered the idea). At the sight of a composer who amasses great instrumental resources, and even great vocal ones, bringing forth a work not in the old form, we will have the courage to ask now, with more chance of a sufficient answer, Whether it is really the power of the inspiration which breaks the form, or simply the *mass of resources?* In the latter case, no phœnix will arise from the extinguished ashes of the old form, but from the broken vase will be given forth a thick, strange mass, which will fall heavily to the ground.

On the other hand, if a really important work comes out victorious from the combat,

7

necessitated by the shallow ideas of its contemporaries, we must forthwith consider the
form and instrumentation as the indispensable
means of conveying the thoughts of the composer. If this form and instrumentation differ
widely from the accustomed form, we can no
longer judge the work by the old rules, but
must search into it to deduct new ones.

No branch of musical art has developed in
such a short time as the symphony, from its
origin to its hitherto unquestioned apogee.

The *lied*, for instance, although it had already found its first great masters at the beginning of this century, exists to-day in new
forms, thanks to the fusion of the word and the
note, adapted entirely to the melodic character
of the *lied*. Numbers of the *lieder* composed since those of Schubert need not fear
comparison with his immortal songs. By the
reformatory action of Wagner, innumerable
roads are open to the musical drama, and each

8

From the water-colour drawing of Wilhelm Rieder.
(By permission of Messrs. Breitkopf and Härtel, publishers of the complete works of Schubert.)

FRANZ PETER SCHUBERT.

composer will take that which best suits his chosen subject. And now let us remember that Haydn wrote his first symphony about 1760, and that in 1823, only sixty-three years later, the transformation of a gay pastime into a sublime tragedy had already taken place—the Choral Symphony had been born. More than three quarters of a century has passed since the appearance of this marvellous work, and still does it wear, in the realm of symphony, the undisputed crown. Almost always the greatest prosperity is followed by a temporary lull, often a complete chaos, and so I believe that in the domain of the symphony, Nature, after having ripened the most remarkable minds in a short space of time, after having produced a Haydn, a Mozart, and finally a Beethoven, has taken a rest, a breathing-spell, after its overwhelming effort. The productive force has all gone in the direction of the opera, towards the musical drama, as in

9

the case of the hitherto unsurpassed Richard Wagner. Is it necessary to deduct from this "an Extinction of Absolute Music from the general domain of the arts," and, in consequence, its right to exist as an absolute art in itself? Does, then, every advance take place only on the birth of a surpassing genius? Such minds can neither be foreseen nor counted upon, and when they do come, they throw every calculation upside down. Therefore, we can never know with what power a coming master may not use the old symphony form. Wagner himself seems later to have retrenched on that opinion so roughly expressed in "Opera and Drama," when in his book, "On the Employment of Music in the Drama" (ten vols. of complete works), he admits, under certain conditions, the possibility of writing symphonies in which something new can still be said. In order to consider this possibility, which is not plainly indicated, we will briefly, without omitting necessary details, review the principal points brought out so far in the domain of the symphony.

Haydn studied the sonatas of Ph. Emanuel Bach, which were freer and less severe than the studies of his renowned father; then later created similar tone pictures for the chapels of the different princely houses at which he was in turn musical director—masterpieces, of which a great many are immortal, they are often so fresh and sunny that it always seems as though we hear them for the first time, genuine outbursts of Haydn's simple, happy nature. Mozart was deeper in sentiment than Haydn. Much more roughly treated in the fight for existence, so that his frail body was prematurely undermined in health, he expresses frequently, in his compositions, the gravity which enveloped his life. The sweet melancholy of the G minor Symphony, the austere severity of the one in C major, the majestic

11

gravity of the first two portions of the one in E flat, are characteristic traits, unknown in the instrumental works of Haydn. But Mozart's peculiar talent shows itself above all in the opera. The phrasing in the last scene of "Don Juan," and in the "Magic Flute," the instructive indications that he gives in his handling of the orchestra in "Figaro," do not appear in his symphonies.

Beethoven, in his first two symphonies, also shows the influence of his predecessors. Had fate so willed it that he had died after having finished the Symphony in D minor, no one would ever have known what power of thought his mind contained. But then a miracle occurred. A great figure in the political world, the First Consul of France, so filled the young musician with enthusiasm, that he determined to glorify him in a great musical poem, and—like Minerva springing from the hand of Jupiter—so was the "Eroïca" symphony conceived.

12

No artist has ever made a step as gigantic as that which Beethoven made between his second and third symphonies. He felt in the depth of his great soul that the ideal existence, freed from the impurity common to all humanity— I might almost say the true life of a hero, and the universal appreciation of his worth—does not take place till after his death. So in the first movement of the symphony only he shows us the hero himself, in the midst of his struggle and powerful efforts, in the fullness of his victorious activity. The second movement already chants the Death Song; the third, that astonishingly short Scherzo, shows us the image of those worldly folk who, always occupied in their little affairs, pass by with scorn, or neglect to see altogether the grandeur and high projects conceived at their very side. Then in the last movement Beethoven shows us the multitudes running from all corners of the earth, all men bringing each their stone, to assist in the erection of a monument worthy of the now universally recognised hero. In boldness of conception and polyphonic execution, this last movement is greater even than the two first, and compared to it the much admired final fugue of the "Jupiter" symphony of Mozart appears only child's play. When finally the veil falls from the monument, shouts of enthusiasm resound, all eyes involuntarily fill with tears, an ecstatic shudder passes over us at the sight of our own idol; the sounds that we hear proclaim that, with this symphony, music has been emancipated, has become a language expressing feelings hitherto considered impossible for it to express. Who is there that does not stop in wonder at Beethoven going from one great work to another, and finally crowning the monument of his creations with the Ninth Symphony! However, it is not of Beethoven himself that I wish to speak; rather of those that came after him. Perhaps I have already wandered too far from the subject of my lecture, but, as when in the course of a journey through the valley (to take up again the metaphor of the commencement), we know that the beautiful snow-capped peak which has excited our astonishment and admiration is going to disappear from before us, we cannot prevent ourselves from turning to it before looking at the smaller hills, so I have not been able to resist the temptation of speaking at length of at least one of Beethoven's works before he disappears from these pages, but to return to view occasionally—in the far distance, as it were.

Turning now our glance from that gigantic mountain, we find, in taking stock of its surroundings, hills of many hues, numerous spots, rocky and romantic, that are capable of interesting and pleasing us. So it is with the symphonies which have been written since Beethoven. There are many beautiful ones and many of incontestable value, but as we turn away from the snow-capped peak, so must we also turn away from the symphonies of Beethoven, in order to see clearly those that have been composed after him.

Quite close to Beethoven, and his contemporary rather than his successor, comes a wonderful musical light—Franz Schubert. No other has, to the same extent, had such a wonderful melodic imagination united to such a rich faculty of musical invention, and such profound and tender feeling.

We find in Beethoven, whenever he lets us see his method of working, a violent struggle toward a determined end, to express his feelings in an adequate musical phrase: Schubert's ideas, on the contrary, flow, as it were, from an inexhaustible source; he gathers them up without distinction, happy in their very existence, and preserves all of them faithfully. It is astonishing that he could write so many

16

works in such a short life. He only lived thirty-one years, but he produced far more than the other great masters of music. His whole being was saturated with melody, so that he produced continually, simply setting down his ideas as they came to him, without retrenching. His was a happy, lovable nature, altogether Viennese in its sentiments, and one which easily over-rode the difficulties of existence. The poverty which he suffered all his life could not silence the Divine Voice within him.* To tell the truth, Schubert's rapid, almost fabulous

---

* This brings to my mind a little anecdote which was told to me in 1886 by Franz Lachner, ex-music director at the court of Munich, who in his youth was Schubert's boon companion. One fine morning Lachner asked Schubert to join a party of friends who were going to make a trip into the country. Schubert wished very much to accept, but having no money, had to refuse. Lachner being also very hard up, it made the case very embarrassing. So Schubert gave Lachner a portfolio of manuscript songs, asking him to sell them, for, he added, he had been so often to the publisher that he dared not go

rate of production had also this disadvantage, that many insignificant and superficial things escaped from his pen, which were not worthy of being handed down to posterity. One must even put amongst these the greater half of his compositions, but those of his works above this average, place him in line with the greatest masters. In a recent article on a modern composer, I saw the assertion that, properly speaking, he was not a genius, not having enriched music by giving to it any new forms.

According to that, Schubert had very little

---

again. The publisher—Lachner said it was Diabelli —proved very angry, exclaiming "Some more of Schubert's stuff!" and stating very seriously that no one would buy Schubert's songs. Finally, however, he gave way, and bought all the manuscripts for five florins! Very happy, the two friends went on their trip, and finding a spinet at the inn at which they stopped, Schubert improvised some more songs, of which he received the inspiration on the road. Unfortunately, Lachner could not remember which they were, but he assured me that one of them is nowadays considered amongst Schubert's most beautiful songs.

himself. Certainly he has given us no new forms, but his rich individuality shows itself in the old ones, and genius lies in such individuality. Schubert was the lyric poet *par excellence.* In his gayest, as in his most tragic works, there is a flow of tenderness and melody through which we always see his inner self, as through a veil of sweet tears. A true heart-lightening warmth is given out from his music.

Do you remember the great C major Symphony? Schubert himself probably never heard it, and it is dreadful to think that it would, perhaps, have remained forever unknown if Schumann had not discovered it at Vienna long after Schubert's death. How grandly it stands before us, with its four monumental movements: the first full of life, of exuberant force, the second of gipsy-like romanticism, with the marvellous, mysterious horn passage (the Celestial Host, as Schumann so beautifully calls it), the charming Scherzo,

19

and the finale of colossal fantasy! No *cherché* harmonic effects, no sort of polyphonic combinations awake our interest, yet this work, though extraordinarily long (one whole hour, without interruption), has captivated us and commanded our admiration. I cannot understand how there can exist people of such cranky humour as to find this symphony too long, and to wish to cut it down. I am not one of those, and I confess that when I hear this work well executed, or when I execute it myself, I experience the profoundest sensation of happiness. This music literally seduces me. The free flight across a light-impregnated atmosphere would, perhaps, produce similar feelings: Nature has refused us this delight; works of art alone can give us them.

What shall I say of the two movements which exist of the Symphony in B minor. In general, it is assuredly unfortunate when an author does not finish his work, but of this symphony I

might almost say it is fortunate that it remained uncompleted. The first movement is
full of a tragic grandeur that, apart from
Beethoven, no other symphonist has been able
to attain; Schubert himself has never raised
himself so high, except in one or two of his
songs. I consider the counter-subject given out
by the 'cellos as one of the most majestic inspirations it has ever been given to a musician
to express. That which in the first movement
gives us the vivid impression of a soul-
struggle, seems in the second an ideal gentle-
ness, as if the musician was already planning
his journey towards eternal rest. For my part,
this ending is so satisfying that I have never
had, after the second movement, the desire to
hear a continuation of the work. One might
think that Schubert wished to finish by the
slow movement, as Beethoven did in the piano-
forte sonatas (Op. 109, 111); but its tonality,
so far removed from the key of the first move-

ment, proves his intention of continuing the symphony. In reality there exists an orchestrated commencement, and a sketch still further advanced, of a Scherzo, belonging to the B minor Symphony; but judging from what does exist, this movement would not have reached the standard of the first two. By the breadth and force of sentiment, united to the tenderly lyric element, which flits across his work like a ray of light, Schubert appears a noble, and somewhat feminine complement of Beethoven. These two great symphonies, in which his rich individuality is so evident, are the only ones which can approach those of Beethoven. In the realm of quartet, the same might be said about those in D minor and G major.

The second great contemporary of Beethoven, the author of the "Freischütz," has left us high-class productions in his piano sonatas, but nothing in the domain of the symphony.

CHAPTER II.

LEAVING Schubert, we now turn to the true post-Beethoven symphonists: first of all, the clever and elegant Felix Mendelssohn. One might say that he disproves the saying that "there is no such thing as a Heaven-born master." He who, at the age of seventeen years, when others are just growing out of childhood, composed the overture of the "Midsummer Night's Dream," was truly a master descended from Heaven. Without doubt, if we consider the elf-dance in Weber's "Oberon," we are of Wagner's opinion that in the "Midsummer Night's Dream" they are not

elves, but flies. However, the perfection of
form, the surety of invention in view of a determined result, and the workmanship that the
composer shows us in this overture, and also in
the string octet (written earlier still—a true
model of beautiful sonority in the use of instruments), all these were attained at such an
early age only by Mozart, and compel our
astonishment and admiration.

From the standpoint of rules, Mendelssohn
had nothing more to learn after writing these
pieces. What he should have possessed in
order to create works equal to those of his
predecessors, he could not obtain. It had to
be in him, and it was not. A distinguished
nature, lovable, poetic, eminently spiritual, reveals itself in all that we know of the man's
character, in his letters and in his music. But
he possessed neither intensity of inward sentiment nor passion. Compare the overture with
the rest of the "Midsummer Night's Dream"

From a pencil drawing by E. P. Novello.

FELIX MENDELSSOHN-BARTHOLDY.

Symphony Writers since Beethoven.

music. The latter was composed four years before Mendelssohn's death, seventeen whole years after the overture. Nearly all the composer's works come between the overture and the rest of the music, and yet it might all have been done at the same time, so little difference can we discern.

On the contrary, compare the works of the other great masters between which there was a long time : for instance, compare the "Flying Dutchman" with "Tristan," Beethoven's First Symphony with the Seventh, and Mozart's "Idomeneo" with the "Magic Flute"; what an immense difference !

Wagner could not, in his Parisian version of "Tannhäuser," express in the language of "Tristan" and the "Ring" the thoughts contained in the earlier work, and, indirectly, it is much to his credit. Mendelssohn did not, like most of his brother creative artists, increase his musical power as he grew older.

From the beginning to the end of his life and production, he remained a "Master descended from Heaven." Whether he wrote piano-pieces, songs, symphonies, oratorios, pieces of opera, always the same perfection of form, the same harmonic disposition in the treatment of the orchestra, the same nobility and freshness were present.

Of his symphonies, two, those in A major and A minor, are often played nowadays. Both owe their birth to the impressions received from nature to which Mendelssohn was particularly sensible.

From that fact they have the advantage over the cold "Reformation" Symphony, and the Symphony of the cantata ("Hymn of Praise"), of having sprung from a live sentiment, thus producing on the public a more lively impression than these two, which to-day are only known by name amongst the works which exist.

26

In these symphonies, as in those of Schubert, the personality of the author is apparent, entire and perfect. The essential difference is in the individuality of the two masters. Raphael paints a Saint Cécile; Jan van Huysen paints a small study of flowers. Genius must not be judged from one standpoint more than another. By genius I understand chiefly the faculty of expressing completely and without restriction, by means of art, one's individuality—a faculty which depends essentially on the purely technical ability; but if that faculty be there, inbred, as it were, one can, and always will, acquire the ability by application. There emanates from the works in question a feeling of mastership based on that true sincerity which does not attempt to give more than it possesses. This sincerity Mendelssohn possessed in a high degree : that is why he appears to us, if not great in what his nature enabled him to give, at least a figure accomplished on all points. That is why his compositions show, in spite of a lack of soul-felt power, that sympathetic perfection which exempts us from asking the HOW, and makes us only take into consideration the WHAT of his artistic personality. His immediate successors cannot pretend to the same degree of talent.

With Mendelssohn began that period of music usually called the Neo-classic. Its representatives continued to respect the firm traditions of the old masters, but they brought into their music a sentimental element tinged with the mystic, which, in contrast with the naïvely objective manner of their predecessors awakes the necessity of a subjective explanation. The legends of chivalry and the Middle Ages are brought back to life. The empire of elves and spirits envelops the ideal of classic beauty in a mist of hallucinations. The so-called metaphysical school was founded at an epoch almost contemporary with our German school of poetry. This Neo-classic period in music has also been called the romantic, and its representatives sometimes go by one name, sometimes by the other. In his small sphere, Mendelssohn has always remained the artist, objective and accomplished; but, by his sympathy for the old masters, he, above all, deserves the name of *Neo-classic*.

The first and most classic characteristic of the subjective romanticists—Weber, who was an objective musician, a romantic classicist, being excepted—was Robert Schumann. His was an individuality diametrically opposite to that of Mendelssohn. In one, all is exterior; in the other, all came from the soul: in one, a natural dexterity from the earliest age; in the other, an everlasting struggle towards the new and perfect, until a melancholy fate put the intellectual powers in fetters. In the first period of his career, we only see Schumann as a composer for the piano. He built his pieces

on poetic pictures; in one case he took for a
theme the name of one he loved in his youth,
and wrote variations upon it. The many
coloured carnival scenes inspired one of the
richest piano compositions that we possess; the
fantastic stories of Hoffman induced the
"Kreisleriana" and the important Sonata in F
sharp minor. For the "two souls within him"
he substituted the two personifications Florestan and Eusebius, and attributed now to one,
now to the other this or that work. Violently
assaulted by the critics and the Incorporated
Association of Musicians, he founded with
several congenial friends the Society of David-
ites, and danced vigorously, gaily on the backs
of the Philistines. Let us state at once, as the
composer for the piano, one might say piano-
poet, he possessed the sincerity of the great
masters, in that he was content to be himself
and showed no inordinate desire to be more
than what he was by nature. New and daring

ideas are expressed in these works, and to-day we accept with extreme pleasure the offering of his rich imagination. His handling of the piano was also quite original. It differed entirely from the accustomed style, and conformed with the spirit of the instrument as well as with the musical thoughts.

It was only when thirty-one years of age that Schumann turned towards the larger forms of his art, such as the symphony. The brilliant figure of Mendelssohn, endowed in all musical branches with a facility which made all his works seem play to him, appeared early as an ideal to the eyes of Schumann, casting its influence on the life and career of the young composer, not, unfortunately, for his good. In his efforts to follow in the traces of Mendelssohn, to attain to the latter's degree of perfection, I might say, to become a classic, his fundamental nature was to some extent damaged, and he could never have equalled his model. A foreign element, as it were, grafted upon him—precisely that Mendelssohnian perfection which he tried in vain to attain— later on took from his works that spontaneity and life-like quality which so charms us in his earlier compositions.

These natural gifts, which, in the smaller forms, produced such excellent results, fell to pieces in the larger ones: the ideas are not any richer; on the contrary, they are more meagre and threadbare: he wished to give more than he possessed. In spite of that, his production was astonishingly large and varied in this second period of his career. There are not, it must be remarked, many forms of music, at which he did not try his hand.

In accordance with his free-thinking tendencies, he had a great antipathy to the idea of composing biblical oratorios. So he chose as subjects, secular poems, such as Goethe's "Faust," and produced works which stand as a sort of compromise between the opera and the oratorio. Besides numerous songs, many of which may be counted amongst the most distinguished ever written, he composed concertos, all kinds of chamber music, musical dramas, an opera, and also, it is unnecessary to add, some symphonies.

Now, I must expect to be considered an arrant heretic, for I am going to confess frankly that I do not count Schumann's symphonies amongst his important works.

In his piano pieces, his characteristic is the invention of little, very expressive themes, which he varied and used in an exceedingly brilliant manner. But in his symphonies he does not come out as well with these little themes, although they often spring from a warm and beautiful sentiment.

If you study in detail his orchestral works, you will find that frequently he had to resort to repetitions of separate bars in order to carry on the thread of his discourse, because the theme is too small. What is more, that theme is often composed of such repetitions.

By such tonic repetitions which, naturally, are also rhythmic, his larger orchestral works easily become monotonous.

One could reply to this theory of mine by saying that the theme of Beethoven's Fifth Symphony is even smaller than those of Schumann, but there is this essential difference between the two : that Beethoven, after the first two short expositions of the four-note subject, handled it so that a distinct and single melody is given out from beyond the organ point in the first violins, and the repetition of the theme on A-flat-F, up to the beginning of the counter-subject (entry of horns in E flat); the theme is only used by the melody as a link of the rhythmic chain, and, properly speaking, it is not necessary for its prolongation; whereas with Schumann, the sound structure is only

34

upheld, in a semblance of solidity, by the repetition of the theme, and the adoption of phrases which often have no *raison d'être* in the organic whole.

This weakness of Schumann is particularly noticeable in his first movements, and even more in the finales of his symphonies, which are noisy and commonplace, with the exception of the one in B flat major, which, though of little importance, is graceful on account of its principal theme. Involuntarily we ask ourselves why the end of a Schumann symphony always engenders a feeling of unhappiness, whereas in a Beethoven symphony such is never the case: the reason is, I think, that in Beethoven's music the happiness results from psychological necessity, from great grief previously conquered, as in the fifth and ninth symphonies, or else is bound in with the fundamental character of the work, as in the Seventh Symphony.

35

The grandiose, broad adagio of Beethoven is replaced in Schumann's works with graceful, pretty intermezzi, which would be much better for the piano than for the orchestra.

Generally speaking, a Schumann symphony produces more effect when well played as a piano duet than in the concert-room. The reason is, as the most fervent admirers of the master dare not refuse to acknowledge nowadays, that Schumann had not the slightest idea of handling an orchestra, either as director or in writing for it. He nearly always employed the full band, seldom trying to group the different bodies of instruments according to the individual "timbre."

With an almost childish lack of skill, he thought he could produce a fullness and power of sound by doubling the parts. His instrumentation became, through this, so thick and dull that if it were played as he marked it, nothing of any meaning would be given out by

36

the orchestra, and it would be as impossible to produce a true *forte* as an expressive *pianissimo.*

Comparing from the standpoint of a conductor. the amount of work required before rendering a Schumann symphony, the difficulty of the study and the number of rehearsals, with the result finally obtained, a feeling creeps over me such as I should experience in the presence of one whose love I was seeking, but could not find. No beauty or light radiates from this dull mass of instruments, which, however, is immediately transformed by the performance, even, of one of Mendelssohn's simplest pieces.

It would seem as if Schumann's symphonies were written for the piano, and arranged, not well, alas!—for the orchestra. Certainly they contain some true flights of genius, beautiful, soul-stirring (because soul-felt) passages, which recall the early period of the composer, as, for instance, in the introduction to the B flat major Symphony, which promises great results. The following first movement falls back again into his customary uniformity of rhythm and tiresome repetitions. The middle movements have more value than the first, except the first trio of the scherzo, which is quite insignificant, and shows up terribly the weakness of Schumann in symphonic writing. The best movement in the four Schumann symphonies, to my idea, is the "adagio espressivo" of the one in C major, with its violin phrase, soaring, as it were, to Heaven, only to descend to earth again almost immediately.

Now, Schumann seems quite different to us, even in orchestral composition, when he follows a poetic impulse in accord with his genius, as in the "Manfred" music, after Byron's poem. Here the wish to be classic did not intrude; he was himself, that is to say, the man of fancy, the romantic, inspired by mystery and the

38

supernatural. In fact, the sympathy of his nature with his subject caused him to succeed in producing a composition which has the right to be called classic. The great "Manfred" overture, with its extraordinary brio, and well enough orchestrated, is, amongst his orchestral music, the only piece worthy to be put on a level with his piano music. As for the rest of the "Manfred music, it shows us that, under certain conditions, even an artistic absurdity like the mélodrame can have an impressive effect when a great genius undertakes to compose it. I refer especially to the "Exorcism of Astarte."

This scene, well rendered by the actor and orchestra, leaves nothing to be desired in its impressiveness; one does not wish that Manfred could really sing here, any more than that in "Fidelio" and "Der Freischütz" the dialogue should be set to music.

I do not wish here to take up the defence of

39

the mélodrame, which appears to be coming back into use, and which is even employed and maintained by the Wagnerians, but it would be ridiculous to condemn the "Exorcism of Astarte" simply because it is a mélodrame.

In these days, when the critics are more than ever given to the ill-treating of works of art, and numbers of so-called "Principles of Art"—in Germany called prejudices— mostly resulting from misunderstanding, or stupid quoting of Wagner's writings, float about in the heads of artists, preventing free power of creation, it cannot be too strongly recommended to them that they train themselves constantly to receive and to put down their natural, unaffected impressions. Then will it be easier for them to know truth from falsity, for in art all rules are futile, only good to show how best they may be broken; living, and of benefit can the work be, only when it is in itself fresh and unrestrained.

From a photo by C. Brasch, Berlin.

JOHANNES BRAHMS.

Wagner's explanatory theory of the Ninth Symphony will never be convincing, though his performance of it, in 1872, has opened up new paths in the art of conducting, which are of great and eternal value. Schumann, who had hitherto encouraged every ideal effort and endeavour, earnestly and lovingly, assumed towards the greatest of his contemporaries, of whose development he was a witness, after a short period of sympathy, an attitude first of indifference, then of enmity even.

Those who love Schumann must try to efface from their minds his unwarrantably prejudiced judgment of " Tannhäuser." He turned completely away from Wagner, and then, in opposition to him, hailed in glowing terms, as a future musical Messiah, a young man who at that time was only known by his piano sonatas. This young musician was Johannes Brahms. By this prophecy of Schumann, one foresees at once that the enemies of the

41

audacious reformer of the opera would take Brahms as a counter-balance, and make him the champion of absolute music against the pro-gramme-music of the future. In reality Brahms owes a great deal of his—I do not say im-portance but—reputation, which, by the way, he made very early in comparison with other composers, to the incessant efforts of a group of Wagner's enemies, who never lost an oppor-tunity of comparing him with the Master of Bayreuth.

This sort of rivalry was absolutely senseless, for, to begin with, the difference between the species of absolute music, such as one attributes to the symphonist, and the musical drama and all other kinds of music, is not so great as one is often inclined to think nowadays, despite Wagner's profound reasoning upon the subject. Moreover, strictly absolute music, that is to say, music manufactured without any moving basis, a mass of notes within the bounds of a certain form, trumpery phrases often escaped from the pen of a Philistine of art, in view of its empty tiresomeness, has no right even to atttention; and it is entirely without importance whether the work is called neo-classic, or modern, or both.

All music must acknowledge the influence of the composer's soul, even when there are no words and no published programme. In this sense, no one of our masters was an absolute musician; Beethoven less than any of them.

There is one more thing which is neglected only too often by those who, taking advantage of their station and the influence of their pen to depreciate and lessen a figure which annoys them, maintain in regard to it the silence of death, while they praise and laud to the skies another who is more to their taste. Such are the party chiefs, who through blind fanaticism or from other motives, give to a certain personality their friendship or their enmity, as

43

an objective valuation of his worth, and wish to mould to their ideas the opinion of the public. This neglected factor is the force of truth, slow moving, to be sure, but everywhere and always triumphant.*

A manufactured, a false success resembles a torrent formed by a heavy shower. There, where usually no water runs, it takes with it in its impetuous rush all that lies in its path, and some few hours after no trace of it can be found. But the real, true success is like the spring starting from the profound depths of the soil. At first it trickles along unnoticed, a tiny stream of water, then becomes a brook, then a river, and, finally, immense, it throws itself into the ocean. No matter how one tried to dam it up, it would always reappear.

---

* I do not direct these and the following remarks against Brahms himself. One had only to know the simple artist to understand how he kept himself aloof from all outside controversy and self-advertisement.

Fortunately, it is already certain that the prejudice of the Brahmsites will never destroy one tittle of the grandeur of Wagner, and without doubt Brahms will also take in the history of art the place he merits, in spite of the much too violent and noisy attacks that the Wagnerians make against him, by way of revenge.

Time is the strictest judge; he eats up what is meant for destruction; only that which is above him, can he not touch.

We cannot say, as yet, with certainty, what height Brahms will reach under the dictum of Father Time, being at present too much under the solemn influence of his death.

Doubtless, also, the figure of Brahms would be more sympathetic to those who are not his blinded worshippers, if two things had never existed : first, this artistic quarrel with Wagner, carried on originally with fervour, and even yet in a half-hearted fashion here and there;

45

then that joke of the three B.'s, invented by Von Bülow, and since become celebrated, which puts Brahms in the same category with Bach and Beethoven. However, this foolishness was only due to a personal motive (perhaps the very reason why it found so many disciples), for —permit me to repeat what so many others have also said—Von Bülow would never have aided the propaganda for Brahms if he had not previously had a rupture with Wagner, a quarrel so painful, and so deeply to be regretted, for the sake of the entire further development of our popular artistic culture.

Here a great and originally noble spirit inclined to a fault which the small and wicked so willingly commit, namely, of elevating to an exaggerated extent the reputation of one artist in order to lower that of another by contrast. Reading Von Bülow's letters, and comparing them to what, in the last fifteen years of his life, he said and did, one can only feel unhappy that a mind and a character like his were doomed to be a stranger to Wagner's work, and thus to the development of the musical art in general, at a time when he would have been of most assistance to it.

We see many other great artists who have much trouble to make themselves seen, through the lack of intelligence and blindness of their contemporaries; they only become known by means of a rousing and agitated fight, which seems, as it were, to place an aureole of glory round their head.

In the case of Brahms, on the contrary, although happily one knows that he took no active part in this dispute, one will be sorry to remember how he was thrown first to one side by one party, then to the other by a celebrated conductor, whose caprices, often most insignificant, were looked upon as prophecies, and that, on both sides, those who glorified him were impelled to do so by their interest in op-

47

posing another greater than himself. Now, I shall try to picture the feelings aroused in me by the compositions of this musician.

When Brahms appeared with his First Symphony, his friends cried "this is the Tenth Symphony." They meant by that, of course, the tenth Beethoven symphony. Putting aside all such exaggeration, I recall the C minor Symphony by Brahms as being a work of sturdy ruggedness, mightily worked out, which corresponded, much more than Schumann's, to my idea of a symphony, and in which the orchestra is also infinitely more cleverly handled. I admire the adagio in the highest degree, and, above all, I like the beautiful slow introduction to the last movement. The horn passage in C major, across a tremolo of the strings coming after the minor, has an extremely stirring effect. It is like the sun shining through a waving morning mist.

Brahms breaks away from the often confused romanticism of Schumann, and approaches more nearly to the energetic plastic expression of the older masters, especially Beethoven. He has succeeded in rivalling it in the first and last movements of the C minor Symphony, making that composition resemble the image one sees of one's self in a concave mirror. His Second Symphony is, to my mind, greatly superior to the first. One can scarcely find any other work of Brahms in which the inventive power has come forth so fresh and original; nowhere has he made his orchestra so sonorous.

The first movement is, from the beginning to its much admired finish, a masterpiece. The second movement one can only understand after repeated hearings; it comes to the ear with difficulty, but it penetrates deeply. If a comparison were allowed me, I should say that it resembled a Dutch landscape, seen at the setting of the sun. At first one sees only the sky above vast plains; the glance, almost weary, goes aimlessly wandering over the picture. But little by little an impression, a picture comes forth—great yet gentle—and touches us. Little by little, also, I have conceived a fondness for this movement, which at first seemed to me insipid; in spite of my sincerest efforts, I have not been able to do as much with many of Brahms's other compositions.

The intermezzo in minuet form is a graceful piece of badinage; it is too small to be in proportion to the other three movements. The finale brings to an energetic close this important work, which I unhesitatingly put above the four Schumann symphonies, and even place amongst the very best of the neo-classic school composed since the death of Beethoven.

In many other works of Brahms, as in the last two symphonies, there is, to my idea, more reflection than true artistic feeling, more of that fanciful element of cunning which was peculiar to him, and from which he could never quite free himself. I shall explain myself more fully on this subject. First of all, I wish to remark that amongst the miscellaneous works of Brahms, there are several which I appreciate as highly as the Second Symphony. Besides certain parts of the German Requiem, I might mention several *lieder*, the "Song of Fate," and several chamber music compositions; but these works are, some of them completely, others more than usually, free from that unnatural, studied element inherent in Brahms, an element which soon became a system.

In speaking of a system peculiar to Brahms, I mean a complication of several ever-returning expedients, which he uses to build up a composition. One of these was his so dearly beloved method of syncopation, that is to say, putting the bass on a later beat than the upper parts, and vice versa, so that one part seems to go limping after the other, so to speak. It is a result peculiar to this syncopation.

Imagine a quite simple melody, formed usually by a progression of crotchets, and accompanied harmonically. Then think of the notes of the bass, not meeting the corresponding notes of the melody, but always placed a quaver's length after them: the general effect has, and that in very rare cases, an appearance of knowledge, but is lacking in true depth of sentiment.

It is just as if one gave oneself airs of great importance while saying the simplest thing in the world: the face does not become really expressive. Another thing that Brahms liked even more was to combine binary with ternary rhythms; for instance, to put triplets opposite a movement of simple quavers, which procedure when prolonged, or employed frequently, gives the sensation of an unpleasant oscillation.

52

Still another custom to make the upper parts, often the middle, and sometimes the bass, move by intervals of thirds, or more frequently still, of sixths, then to throw all the parts *pêle-mêle* into the most ingenious web of syncopation. There are entire portions of this work built in this manner.

We frequently find phrases, even the formation of themes, composed of the fifth of the common chord below the tonic combined with the third above, and the next superior fifth, always avoiding the fundamental note. We find this so often that the sketch was once called by a very clever wit while speaking to me of Brahms, his "leading motive."

Study the compositions of Brahms, especially those habits of which I have been speaking; you will at least find confirmation of these facts, although many, perhaps most of you, will see nothing of importance in my deductions therefrom.

I consider that that melodic and harmonic complexity (called depth of sentiment by the Brahmsites), which results from the above-mentioned mannerisms, and which, of course, destroys the clearness of the music, is the cause of so many of Brahms's compositions giving the impression of forced and anti-natural works, that all the technical skill in the world cannot make capable of warmth. It cannot be denied, either, that precisely this complexity engenders a monotony which is absolutely foreign to a real and true simplicity. The latter will always and everywhere be happy in its effects; it will always appear new and young. After a hundred changes of opinion, we still admire it to-day in Mozart and Haydn.

Monotony, on the contrary, especially when it springs from too much complexity as in

Brahms, certainly induces at first reflection and research, but in the long run it becomes fatiguing, and ends by producing that dangerous poison which kills art, and which everyone tries to avoid like death itself—ennui.

It is very rarely that the compositions of Brahms are really simple, but when they are, they are very beautiful. Take as instances "La Solitude des Champs," the "Sapphic Ode," and the first movement of the "German Requiem." If you notice, when he wished to write simply, a wish aroused by, it seems to me, an inordinate desire to be popular, his invention becomes insignificant, without importance, and recalls the feeble "Songs without Words" of Mendelssohn; take, for example, the C minor movement of the Third Symphony.

A French critic once wrote about him: "Il travaille extrêmement bien, avec des idées qu'il n'a pas." That is without doubt too severe, but when sometimes, after thoughts and portions really majestic, the musical structure is disturbed and tortured by syncopations, continual meeting of unlike rhythms, progression of thirds and sixths; when following that there arrives, in spots, this artificial simplicity, it seems as if the composer himself wished to arrest, as it were, the flights of his genius: one might say that feeling a betrayal of his utmost feelings, he holds himself back, and envelops himself in a mysterious silence, rather leaving it to be guessed what he wishes to give, than giving it in reality.

It is unfortunate that one is able to point out one certain system as being peculiar to a composer. Would it have been so with the old masters? The symphonies of Haydn certainly resemble each other, yet they are quite distinct one from the other. Then, what a gulf between the "Wedding of Figaro" and the "Magic Flute"? And who could speak seriously of Beethoven's or Wagner's system?

If you do not believe me, try to parody these masters, that is to say, try to represent in an exaggerated style what, according to you, is their system. You would not succeed at all, or you would turn out something heavy and solid without life; to take, say, one of Wagner's themes, and make from it a march, or a set of quadrilles, would be a blasphemy, not a parody. It is very easy, on the contrary, to parody Brahms; Moritz Moszkowsky, for instance, has already succeeded brilliantly in doing so, which, by the way, is like making an imitation of himself. When we hear modern chamber music, composed by disciples of Brahms, we should often take it for that master's work, if we were not beforehand told whose it was; whereas if we heard a fragment of an unknown opera by one of the younger German musicians, no one, I believe, would take it for Wagner.

Face to face with the personality of Brahms, I am not content to close my ears and quote from certain writings of Wagner, as do so many of the latter's disciples. I have played and studied zealously the greater portion of his works. I could always arrive at the meaning of his music without much trouble. I can admire the work, the construction, but I experience a sentiment similar to that of a doctor when dissecting a body well put together. Excepting the works which I have mentioned particularly before, when I let Brahms's music act on me insensibly, I feel the same powerless frigidity that that doctor would feel in making himself try to put life back into the dissected corpse. Brahms was, above all, a master of form. His works are of an unimpeachable technical perfection, but I have only discovered a warm, palpitating feeling of life in very few of them, which then have a great value, owing to the junction of beautiful

58

thoughts and a perfect construction. One feels at once in these cases that the composer has given a loose rein to his individuality. Such being the case, why did he so often check his natural impulse? I seem to hear a voice replying: "As Schumann announced, and his partisans proclaimed later, Brahms believed himself to be the Messiah of absolute music, the successor of Beethoven. He wished to write down this fact in his works." Even in his First Symphony, I recognise an exterior similarity to Beethoven; in other places we often see him not exactly plagiarise from him, but imitate very closely the style of the master's third period, the same rough and daring harmonic progressions, the same opposing rhythms (developing with Brahms into his typical syncopation), and often the same bold melodic leaps. But apart from the natural results of these imitations, they do not resemble each other; it was not given to Brahms to possess

59

the spiritual grandeur of Beethoven. We see from this, that despite the similarity of their outward appearances, it is the essence of music itself which is to be found in Beethoven, in Brahms it is only the idea.

Taken altogether, Brahms's is, I might say, scientific music, composed of sonorous forms and phrases; it is not the language of humanity, mysterious, but still infinitely expressive and comprehensible; it is not the language which the great masters knew how to speak, and did; the language, in fact, which moves and stirs us up to the depth of our being, because we recognise in it our own joys and sorrows, our struggles and our victories. The music of our great masters is artistic, and as such, natural: that of Brahms is artificial It is not related to Beethoven's music, rather is it its antipodes; it is precisely what Beethoven's music is not. Its character is entirely abstract, which is the cause of its imparting that freezing effect to all who would wish to approach it.

As a characteristic experience, I will state that the works of Brahms which attract me the most, such as, for instance, the Symphony in D major, are not esteemed as the summit of his creative power by his enthusiastic partisans. They give the preference to several others, such as the "Song of Triumph," the Fourth Symphony, the Quintet with clarinet, which to me are loud-sounding, empty hollowness. It is precisely to such cold creations—no longer spontaneous, on the contrary, so much reflected over and mannerised, that the author even went out of his way to avoid any sensuous musical charm, either melodic or instrumental —that Brahms owes the reputation of not having been a supporter of the "Modern Heresies."

He was the last to whom this glory will accrue.

New ideas in music have sprung up. New sentiments have marked out for themselves a fresh path; new figures have recommenced with the conservatives, the dispute relative to the classic ideal of form. We can only say to-day that the former have been successful.

Before passing on to the study of this modern branch, I must first mention several composers who, though doubtless influenced by it, yet cannot be said to absolutely belong thereto. They might be called the by-path joining the two roads.

In these last ten years has been often mentioned a powerful rival of Brahms, born in the former's second fatherland, in that city of Vienna which seems to be the city of the symphony. Though much older than Brahms, Anton Brückner, recently deceased, only became universally known even later than him.

What first strikes one about this musician, is the wonderful abundance of new ideas, the individuality of his themes, and the astonishing long-windedness of his melodies.

His was a musical talent, veritably rich. For that reason, one would be almost tempted to compare him to his great compatriot, Schubert, if only he had created works perfect enough to be considered really masterly. But it was not so.

With him, unfortunately, the skill of developing his ideas, of placing one in contact with the other, of establishing them organically, so as to form a complete musical work, did not come up, in value, to his faculty of invention itself.

I cannot bring myself to say, with his pupils and admirers, that he was a great contrapuntist. However, perhaps he was as a professor.

In his compositions the technique is often clumsy, and the polyphonic web obscure and faulty. His marvellous themes seem rather like separately threaded pearls, than like pearls

63

all united on a single cord. This explains why Brückner is left often forceless in the finales of his symphony, instead of reaching there the highest elevation; his last movements are always weaker than the first, which is not favourable to the success of his works.

That explains also why his compositions are mostly cut short and fragmentary, having in consequence an amateurish appearance.

One is tempted to wish that the construction of his work had been less spontaneous, but developed more logically, with more unity, with a determined end in sight. On account of his lack of skill, the grandest thoughts were carried away by the wind, into the waste, for they only make their appearance to remain unrealised.

We feel this sentiment the more, in that many of Brückner's themes bear the stamp of the Wagner "leitmotiven"; so that the truly psychological realisation of the Wagner themes

64

By kind permission of " Die Musik," Berlin.

ANTON BRUCKNER.

Symphony Writers since Beethoven.

stands before us on hearing a Brückner symphony, often inciting us to comparisons.

Brückner, also, inclined slightly to mannerism; the ending of an oft-repeated passage, in the bass, like that of the first phrase of the Ninth Symphony, certain passages with slow movements which sound strangely empty (his admirers say "Weldentruckt"), two similar thematic figures moving simultaneously in contrary motion, as if reflecting each other, and, finally, the truly intolerable rests and organ points, which generally give the impression that he has lost the thread of his discourse, are to be found in all his works with which I am acquainted.

Though we cannot abstain from making these reflections and reproaches in regard to the compositions of Brückner, that does not prevent us from deeply respecting and loving him, above all on account of his grandiose idealism, absolutely incomprehensible nowadays.

Imagine to yourselves this professor, this organist, born in the most needy circumstances and blessed with nothing but a very ordinary education. Without hesitation, he composed symphonies of lengths unheard of almost before; symphonies bristling with difficulties and anomalies of all sorts, which the indolence of conductors, orchestral players, listeners and critics held in terror.

Although knowing from the first that he was not appreciated, he never hesitated a moment even in thought, but remained faithful to his original idea, and did not erase a bar.

Let us compare Brückner to the so-called fashionable composers, borne up by *réclame*, and always looking for a refined effect, and let us incline our heads before his figure, so great and touching in its simplicity: let us erect to him a monument in our hearts. I confess that in modern symphonies, nothing moves me so much nor fills me with so much delight, as a simple theme, a few phrases from Brückner. I recall especially the commencement of the Romantic Symphony.

Certainly the charm diminishes in the course of the work, and vanishes more and more the longer one studies it, for even that which seems at first great and beautiful, can only continue to captivate us when enclosed in an artistically perfect form.

I was once asked my opinion of the rivalry of Brückner and Brahms. I replied, "I should like Nature to give us a musician reuniting in himself the qualities of the two composers, the immense imagination of Brückner, with the knowledge of Brahms. From such a combination would arise an artistic figure of the highest possible value."

Here I must also make mention of another artist who is closely related to Brückner by his noble and elevate ideal; that is the nephew and friend of Wagner, Alexander Ritter, who, to my way of thinking, is more to be esteemed as a poet, in his two one-act operas, than as a dramatic and symphonic composer.

Among the other German composers, I may first name Joachim Raff, who was extremely prolific. Amongst his principal works are the symphonic poem, "Im Wald," and the dramatic "Lenore."

After him comes Robert Volkmann, who, especially in his B flat Trio, has created a work of the highest quality.

Then Felix Dräsecke, first of all quite *modern*, but long since become reactionary. Lastly, I come to Hermann Götz, prematurely deceased, who, from the beauty of his soul, might be the counterpart of Peter Cornelius, the poet musician. It is incomprehensible that his delightful opera-comique, "Der Widerspanstigen Zähmung," shculd have entirely

68

disappeared from the repertoire; it is equally so that one should never see on concert programmes his Symphony in F major, that composition "springing from the quiet and holy spaces of the heart," as Götz himself says in his epigraph.

In Germany, many of the leading musical personalities seize greedily upon every possible superficial work brought from foreign countries, and only known through the medium of skilful advertising, at the same time neglecting national creations full of value. Would a like heresy be possible in any other country able to pride itself on possessing a Hermann Götz, even among the stars of the second magnitude? Will it ever be different?

Such is the question, plaintive and threatening, which has already been asked so often; not often enough, however; such is the appeal made direct to those from whom one would wish to receive a practical response.

I wish to speak now of several really important symphonies by foreign composers, and mention several of them separately, for though worthy of better treatment, they have been, up to now, but little appreciated, and the example I give in playing them has been little followed.

The newest of these creations is the D minor Symphony of the Dane, Christian Sinding. Born of a mysterious northern romanticism, it is often of an abrupt bitterness, and a hardy, daring flight.

The E minor Symphony, by Alexander Borodine, is the most important work I know of in the modern Russian school.

It is masterly, spontaneous, and stamped with the true national character. It stands out strongly, and is absolutely characteristic, and I think, although I never was in Russia, that one could imagine very exactly what the country is, on hearing this composition.

More fortunate as to public acknowledgement than those just mentioned are the Frenchmen, César Franck and Camille Saint-Saëns. The former in his D minor Symphony created a work of real importance; the latter has, with great success, invaded the kingdom of the symphony and the symphonic poem. Other remarkable works composed of late in France, are those of the earnest Vincent d'Indy, under the influence of modern German music. Much interesting matter is offered by the compositions of the young Russian, Alexander Glazounow. The symphony by the young Bohemian, Joseph Suk, is a work full of freshness and spontaneity.

Through his "Village Wedding" symphony, Carl Goldmark is much better known than the two composers I have just named. But they are not villagers whom we see in this symphony, only refined townsfolk, who have taken into their heads to celebrate the wedding of a couple of their friends in the country; throughout we breathe the scent of great *salons* in a composition which should be pastoral in quality. Apart from that, Goldmark's work is brilliant and interesting; it is worthy of being played, and of receiving general approbation.

Let us now mention the honest effort of Anton Rubinstein to reawake the classic symphony to new life, an effort in which he only succeeded once, viz., in a few phrases of his Ocean Symphony, after the most wearisome struggling with the lack of musical feeling.

The "Pathétique" Symphony of Tchaïkovsky, has these last two years, run with great success in the German concert halls. It has also drawn attention to the earlier works of the composer. It is like a theatrical piece, rich in effective and exciting situations, of which the effect on the public is never lacking. Of this work, one of the latest of his compositions, Tchaikovsky himself expresses the fear that it will not be taken for a symphony. For, really, the usual

From a photo by Reutlinger, Paris.

PETER ILJITSCH TCHAIKOVSKY.

Fig. 4. PORTRAIT OF MELANCHOLY.

form is here abandoned, not only in the connection of the movements, but in the separate structure of each. In the first movement, the sonata form is visible, though disguised under a cloak of freedom. The middle movements are more bound by the laws of form : the last is again quite free. Besides, it has the feeling of an adagio, and the symphonic adagio should come in the middle. The inward impulse brings about an ending lost in the most sombre shadows. It is said that a presentiment of death suggested the work to the brain of Tchaïkovsky; he was therefore led away from the form by poetic thought, which attracted, or rather dominated him. In consequence, this will serve us as a stepping stone to the second part of this lecture, the study and analysis of programme music.

CHAPTER III.

JUST about the time that Beethoven died, there appeared among our Western neighbours, in France, a remarkable personality, of whom the grandeur and high value to music have only of late been recognised. This was Hector Berlioz. The first of his works which revealed to us his individuality, the "Symphonie Fantastique" (Op. 14, I think), encloses so great an amount of originality, that one cannot be surprised at his being treated with scorn as a monster, even by men as eminent as Cherubini: as has often been explained, the public could not

74

understand it, and therefore it produced rather a sort of fear, an incomprehensible terror.

This is the less astonishing, in that the general and persistent tendency is to ignore, or deny as being true, everything that is new, rather than to examine the work itself with care, and according to its own sentiment. As long as he lived, Berlioz produced much the same impression, even with his later works, although the tireless efforts of Liszt in their favour drew towards them some attention, at least in Germany. Only long after the death of Berlioz, good productions of his works, well rehearsed, were organised; first by Von Bülow, later by other *chefs d'orchestre.*

But now, at last, the delicate kernel has been discovered behind the rough, hard shell, and the extreme worth of this music is at last felt and understood, standing out from a multitude of seemingly artificial devices. Now that we are familiar with Berlioz, we ask ourselves how it was possible to consider works which are so admired, and excite such enthusiasm nowadays, as the offshoot of a half crazy brain. Three things will explain this.

First of all, the invention of Berlioz appears to us, at first sight, dry and inaccessible. No isolated, melodic phrases stand out in forcible characters, like, for instance, the celebrated clarinet melody in the "Freischütz" overture, or some of Schubert's themes, which insinuate themselves into the ear and heart of the hearer. With Berlioz we seem to experience a sensation of cold, of hardness, where in reality a burning and ardent flame found its musical expression. His music resembles those singular human faces, which at first appear to us antipathetic, then, on considering them more minutely, we understand to what inward storms, what battles of the soul, those hard lines, those scars, those eyes of terrifying profundity bear witness.

76

Look at a portrait of Berlioz to understand what I mean.

Another reason why Berlioz has remained so long misunderstood is the abnormal, grotesque daring of his instrumentation. Not only that he often made use of a much more numerous orchestra than usual, but the manner in which he employed it, the effect he produced with single instruments, the way he handled and combined the different timbres, all give to his orchestration that individual colouring which did not exist before him, and has never been imitated since, it is this colouring which caused unintelligent and spiteful critics to say that he first invented the instrumentation, then added the music. However, his orchestration does not present that material element which forces us to enter, so to speak, into the musical sentiment, and carries us away on its waves; that element, peculiar to the orchestra of Weber also, handled with a boldness worthy of admiration, and, equally so, to the orchestra of Wagner. We are dazzled by Berlioz's instrumentation, not intoxicated; it is a bright sunbeam on the tender green leaves, among which a light, fresh breeze is blowing; it lacks the deep breath of the wind in a forest of pine trees.

The third cause which renders the comprehension of Berlioz so difficult to the majority, is to be found in the peculiarity of the subjects chosen by him for his works; in the way in which the music connects with those subjects; and in the manner of personifying them.

In his "Symphonie Fantastique," in front of which we shall make our first stop, Berlioz has headed each separate movement by a sort of programme, indicating the poetic idea which should be aroused in the mind of the audience. This is not in the least extraordinary. It would be a good thing if some musical historian would firmly establish the fact that

78

what is to-day lightly called "programme-music" is not at all a new idea; on the contrary, the tendency to express clearly indicated thoughts in music is as old as the ordinary forms, as we know them. In the works of the old Dutch and Italian schools, and among the German masters before Bach, we find compositions with titles and explanations.

In his excellent biography of Beethoven, Thayer mentions the existence, at the beginning of the century, of a whole series of compositions, long since forgotten, which had a general title, and each piece a separate name. For instance, "A Naval Fight" for the first: "Beating of the Drums" for the second: "March and Martial Music" for the third: "Movement of the Ships," "Crossing the Waters," "Cannon Shots," "Cries of the Wounded," "Shouts of Joy and Victory from the Triumphant Fleet," and so on. Generally great battles, or important political events, have excited the imagination of the musicians contemporary with them. Beethoven himself did not disdain to celebrate the victory of Wellington, and in Wagner's "Kaisermarch" we hear the echo of a war crowned with success.

The following programme quoted by Thayer, appears to us particularly curious. "The joyousness of life interrupted by a passing storm, then, after it is over, happiness and joy again resume their reign." Who does not recognise the inspirative factor in the composition of the Pastoral Symphony?

Thayer then says very truly : "The ambition of Beethoven was not so much to find new forms, as to surpass his contemporaries in those that already existed." To tell the truth, each good overture has its programme in the libretto of the opera itself, and besides that, Spohr, for one, did not fear to precede his "Faust" overture by a detailed picture of what the listener should hear in the piece. Following

CHARLES CAMILLE SANT-SAENS.

up this subject, I will say also that it is not the *programme* which spoils the music, but the fact that when a piece of this kind is intended to express sentiments which it cannot return to the hearer, it revolts, so to speak, against its own nature, converts itself into "non music," and then it is impossible that a work of art can be born.

The "Symphonie Fantastique" is supposed to represent the feverish dream of a young artist, who, in despair at being rejected by his beloved, poisoned himself with opium; the dose was too weak to be fatal, and he sees passing before him pictures of all kinds, first pleasant, then fearful. The separate movements, each explained very precisely in the programme, are entitled "Dreams and Passions," "The Ball," "Pastoral," "The March to the Scaffold," "Dream of a Witch's Orgie."

Later, Berlioz added a second part, the melo-drama "Lélio," of much less value than the symphony, in which he causes the young artist to awake from his sleep, and speak; and, by repeating in himself his creation, makes plain to us the setting free of his thoughts of love.

One can imagine how the public of that time was incredulous and disconcerted in face of such an undertaking as to set a like subject to music. But how splendidly has Berlioz succeeded in his seemingly impossible attempt! He succeeded without injuring in the slightest the form of the symphony, and without making it into an empty volume of sound. Each of the five movements is complete in itself, pleasing in invention, in construction, in orchestration, and there is no other explanation necessary to account for the existence of these pieces.

Understanding perfectly the purely musical perfection of his work, Berlioz says also that the programme can be omitted when the symphony is played by itself, because the public should understand it without a programme; only the titles of each movement should be left. If an audience gifted with a little imagination knows that the third piece is called "Pastoral," it will recognise easily that the "cantilena" of the English horn at the end of the movement, accompanied by light rolling of kettle-drums, represents the piping of a shepherd, interrupted by distant thunders, just as in Beethoven one recognises the singing of the birds in the Pastoral symphony.

Neither of these imitations is anti-artistic, as they were often called during the composers' lives. They spring from a condition of mind absolutely in touch with the feeling of the music which contains them, from a mind capable of receiving deep impressions from nature, and of giving them their artistic expression. Besides, in both cases, the bars which thus imitate the sound of nature are bound to the preceding ones musically and logically;

they are therefore the outcome of the music itself, without need of knowing the programme; in Berlioz, the imitation of nature offers a good opportunity to perfect the form. While the commencement of the phrase, before the entry of the real theme, is formed by the duet of two pastoral pipes (oboe and cor anglais), the end appears only as a varied resumé of the beginning, so that the beginning and the end interlace, so to speak, and form a frame for the delicate picture expressed in music.

So also, for the last movement—consisting of an introduction which leads to a phrase of mournful character, played by the low brasses (a parody on the "Dies Iræ"), and a fugue, a magnificent piece of work, of which the climax is the union of a choral with the fugue subject, the title of "A Dream of a Witch's Sabbath" would have completely sufficed. Only perhaps, if the public had nothing but

84

the titles, they would not understand the connection between the first three movements and the last two. For this reason, the programme which desires that one regard the work as a painting of an ecstatic dream, should be distributed at executions of this work, the more so that the musical character of the work will not cause it to distract the imagination, but will rather stimulate it, which is the idea of the title.*

If we examine minutely the musical contents of this work, we shall find, as a decided innovation, taking the symphonies up to that

---

* Liszt, in his piano setting of the "Symphony Fantastique," has modified the programme : he marks the first three numbers as natural events, and only the last two as being the outcome of a brain rendered insane by a dose of opium, taken with suicidal intention. I do not consider this change good, as it thus divides the work into two parts. The finely sensitive will interpret the last two movements rather as the development of the fundamental idea than as an entirely new and foreign idea.

time, that a single theme runs through the whole five movements !

In his dream, which the symphony represents in music, the young artist was pursued without rest by the image of his beloved, who appears to him in all sorts of surroundings and different aspects. This image takes the character of what Berlioz calls the "fixed" idea. Thus, while guarding the construction as to the intervals between the notes, it changes completely in rhythm and expression.

In the first movement, the "fixed idea" is given out in a noble simplicity (Breitkopf and Härtel score, p. 10). In the second, "The Ball," it appears enveloped in the strains of a waltz, but quite in the foreground (p. 40). Adapted to the character of the "Pastoral," it is represented by a passage in the wood-winds (p. 66). In the fourth movement it appears only as a fugitive thought of him who was being taken to the place of torture

(p. 94). And lastly, in the last movement, " The Dream of a Witch's Sabbath," it appears as a dance melody, disfigured and grotesque. The well-beloved has become a diabolical harlot, joining in the dances of the witches and fantastic spirits (p. 100 and 104).

It was not through chance, or lack of imagination, as is sometimes pretended nowadays, that Berlioz built with one theme all the movements of this symphony, only the different aspects of the theme are intermingled in the pieces, otherwise independent of each other. To vary and develop a theme is not a new idea; we know that the earlier masters, Beethoven and Schubert before all, have produced many of their masterpieces in the form of variations; we know that in our day Brahms was extremely successful in that form of music. But the variation of a theme resulting from a recognised poetic impulse, the dramatic-psychological variation, one might call it, was employed for the first time in this symphony of Berlioz, and it appears to me to be his own original creation. It is the same kind of variation that Franz Liszt used and perfected in his symphonic-poems, and later that Wagner transformed into a means of such intense expression in his dramas. These Wagnerian themes, varied in accordance with the psychological requirements, are now called "conducting motives."

Here is the opportunity to say that this expression is as lacking in meaning and insipid as the majority of these so-called *leit motiven* themselves. A motive intended to conduct us, to keep us, so to speak, in the right path, so as not to lose ourselves in the labyrinth of music, such as the Wagner scores seem at first glance, such a motive, in order to be recognised without hesitation, should never change.

But the Wagner themes are continually

transformed, one springing from another in the most varied application, just as in our life the ideas of our brain and will become transformed. From this incessant changing they are then but little calculated to lead the ignorant across an obscure domain. It is true that by these very transformations and combinations, only thus possible in the polyphonic character of the music, they become a veritable union of the souls of the acting personages, and that this sort of thematic treatment gives to the Wagnerian music-drama its exciting form and clearness of meaning.

The leading motives with their designations and the "guides" their escort, have made Wagner's music more foggy and indistinct than they have made the meaning clear, for very often people consider that they have sufficiently studied the work when they have discovered the greatest possible number of motives, just as those who look for the greatest number of figures think they have done well enough when they have learnt by heart, through these guides, the specified motives; they lose themselves in subtleties, they rejoice in a feat of memory, without reflection, instead of studying the works more profoundly.

I am willing to admit, however, that the guides have been of much use to those who were intelligent enough not to stop at that point. But nowadays the *leit-motiven* system is brought into all kinds of music, even into the classic symphony form; and the most recent offshoot of it is the analytical-programme book, which is used at orchestral concerts in many places. The intellectual harm that these books do to the listener is far greater than the material benefit that they bring to the publisher. There would be nothing to object to in programme-books filled with musical illustrations, written by a good musician,* above all, about new works, if only one could force the public to read them over before the execution of the pieces.

It is true that at home one has not the opportunity, but in the hall, people spend the time before the beginning of the concert and during the pauses in conversation; and in consequence the books are only read when once the music has commenced. Let us watch a group of listeners, furnished with programme-books; for economical reasons, they naturally look, three or four, over one book; is it not funny to see all the heads joining together, and fingers pointing out the musical example illustrating the phrase that the orchestra is playing? And when the phrase is finished, to see them rush through the text, in order not to lose the next example.

---

* I may mention those of A. Heinz and H. Riemann.

What value can such an insufficient glance have for anyone?

It makes the understanding easier, they reply!

Through this so-called facilitation in understanding, it will some day come about that it will only be necessary for a *chef d'orchestre* to accentuate to the best of his ability the passages marked in the programme-book, in order to get a reputation for "the clearness with which he renders the music." The listener will only have to know these passages, to have a quotation always ready, be able to put in his word, and pass for a connoisseur. Little by little, what idea will a younger generation have of Beethoven?

I never lose any opportunity of pointing out the damage done to the intelligent listener's comprehension by these books. If you do not think that you can dispense with them, then in your own interest, read them as much as possible, before the concerts, at home, and at the same time study the score, or a good arrangement for the piano, of the work.

Then there is another bad custom, resulting from the *leit-motiven* system; that is the search for plagiarism, which has become so widespread in these days. As we are trained by reading programme-books and guides to hear and look at the works, not in their entirety, but in detail, it is only the small minority who, on hearing a new composition, consider the general impression of the whole on themselves, before commencing to consider the details; yet these latter can only be comprehensible by, and in view of, the ensemble.

We look at once for the themes, the "leading motives," with which the piece should be built up; and often, having found them, or perhaps even before they start out delicately and gently from a little guide, like the eyes of a carp from its head, we compare them with other musical examples, seen in other programme-books, principally, of course, with Wagner's themes, for he is the nearest to us, and is the most powerful figure of the recent past.

For this reason, young authors must surely be copyists of Wagner before all others. Bad luck to them if a similarity of two notes should be discovered, if, for example, in one place there is a CG, and in a theme of Wagner's there is a CG also, from that moment the theme is the "Fatal desire motive of Tristan and Isolde," two discomposed fourths, the "start motive," the blows of the cane on Beckmesser, and a dotted $\frac{6}{8}$ rhythm, the pliant "forge motive" of Alberich; in a word, all the work is put down to the god—Wagner. It is astonishing how soon a novelty can be killed; generally without being studied at all as to its real worth. If in Wagner nothing, or too little, is found, in order that the sacrifice to the great man should be sufficiently suspected, we look up Liszt, Wagner's father-in-law, and Berlioz, and then the old masters, and even Meyerbeer, in his trivial operas and songs, for the inspiration of the plagiarist. It would be no small task to gather together the longest experiences and examine closely all the absurdities that this searching brings out.*

In their half childish, half malicious joy at finding such similarities. these reminiscence-hunters forget to consider accurately the character of the theme itself, the place it occupies, the manner of its treatment—to cut matters short, the image, quality and general

---

* A funny man, has, for instance, quoted the theme in the finale of the " Götterdämmerung " on Brünn-hilde's words as " being stolen from an old couplet popular in Germany." There is, it is true, a similarity of notes, but the eyes of the happy revealer must have been very sharp to detect it. On the other hand, it has been sufficient that there is a short tremolo of the strings on A, E, and D, A, for it to be discovered that the Tragic Overture of Brahms is related to Beethoven's Ninth Symphony.

95

appearance of the whole work. They hear with the eyes, not with the ears. They forget that a similar progression of sounds is far from being a plagiarism, that there are many other circumstances which must be considered, such as the movement, the tonality, and the expression, the arrangement as a whole, and, above all, that inward perceptible cause from which springs this particular progression, and not another; they forget all that, because for them such similarity only shows the incapacity of the composer, to find in his own soul the required expression, and the necessity, which this incapacity involves, of hanging himself on to some one else's originality. But they forget also that the reminiscence can be engendered by the disposition of the whole of a passage, and the remembrance of a similar sentiment, without one being able to discover the slightest identity of notes.

It is curious to notice that those similar

From a photo by Nadar, Paris.

FRANZ LISZT.

spiritual dispositions are much less frequently remarked, although they are infinitely more important than proving the dependence of the composer upon accidental notal analogies.

These latter are to be found in large numbers in the greatest masterpieces, from Bach to Wagner : they always remain unperceived, and it formerly never occurred to anyone to criticise a work unfavourably on that account.

Who, for instance, in the time of Beethoven, would have reproached him with lack of originality in the "Eroïca" symphony, because the first theme is similar to notes in the beginning of Mozart's "Bastien and Bastienne"? That Giant Figure was frequently misunderstood, his absence of form-sense, his emphasis, his exaggerated effects, etc., were lamented; but Beethoven would have had to live in our days in order to be treated as a plagiarist because of those similarities.

Thanks to the non-existence of "leading

97

motives," "guides" and "programme-books,"
people knew in his time how to listen to a work
as a whole, as a complete production of the
soul of the composer, not as a collection of
arbitrary details. In a word, they knew that
one had to learn to know a work before criti-
cising it.*

---

* You must agree with me that our opinion of a
piece of music easily changes when we hear it repeated, and that it may do so still more when we
have the score before our eyes, and can study it. The
more prudent, therefore, one gets, and the more
one considers the responsibility incurred in giving a
fixed judgment, the more astonished one is at the
assurance with which so-called professional critics—
excepting, of course, an honourable few—after having
carelessly listened to a piece once played over, write
down a thoughtless criticism which becomes repro-
duced a thousand-fold in the public opinion. What
mistakes are liable to be made, even in the best cases,
where education and honesty are united in the person
of the critic. But there is no limit to the personal
spite possible when both these requirements are lacking. The uneducated critics are well aware that a
remedy for their evil-doing is not possible, as long
as art-criticism exists in its present form, as long
as the critic has not even time properly to hear the

If a composition reflects the evident soul-condition of the author, if the whole and the parts which form it are of a decided and accomplished form, an accidental resemblance of notes to some passage in another work is absolutely without importance.

I say this as clearly and as sharply as possible, firstly, in the interest of composers, who, by the judgment of these reminiscence hunters,

---

piece of which he is going to write, much less to study it: whilst the medium of the press is open to such lost souls, as, not being able to succeed with any original work, find in the pennies they receive per line, a compensation for their incapacity, and so turn their venomous gall against those who tower immeasurably above them, while covering with praise those, who, by their inferiority, are their own kinsmen. Some flatter everybody alike.

I do not think of beginning a useless war against the institution of criticism, as Don Quixote waged war against the windmills, but I content myself with giving this advice to the thinking part of the public : do not believe every word you see against a work because it is printed; rather form your own opinion of the work heard, thus making it possible for you to criticise even the criticism.

run the danger of being turned from the course of their natural instincts : for another reason, as a warning to those who, for fear of this judgment, hurriedly put away from their ideas (perhaps natural and good) any simply innocent consonance, and so give to their work the stamp of a *cherché* originality.

Nothing is more annoying than that, for from it result those agglomerations of high-sounding phrases, of worked out notes, with their superficial feeling, and their subtle banalities, which we see nowadays everywhere, as much in ordinary songs as in the symphony or opera. It is one of the causes of that nervous, sickly musical feeling of our epoch, which has need of the strongest expressions in order to be shaken for a moment from its dreamy sleepiness, only falling back again at once, its glassy eyes shut, into its sleepy lethargy.

I do not even believe I am going too far

in saying that the fear of not being original is the bad spirit which destroys in many of our young composers the feeling and consciousness of good sense, of force and sincerity. It does not annoy me in the slightest that I am reproached with protecting plagiarism, if only I can cry openly and without restraint, "Better an acknowledged reminiscence than an act against nature."

In any case, one can say as a consolation, that reminiscence hunting is only a fashionable disease, which, if it does for the moment attack many intelligent people, will one day disappear, like all fashionable diseases.

However, many creative artists of the present time will perish through it, for everyone has not the force to support calmly its undoubtedly disagreeable effect; everyone has not enough presence of mind to hold up bravely in the face of the demon, " fear of unoriginality ';" and, finally, everyone has not the good sense to honour with a shrug of the shoulders this absurd chase and search for reminiscences, when, on occasion, it appears necessary to say a few effective words on the subject.

It is, without doubt, to Hector Berlioz that the glory of the discovery of that which I have called the psychologico-dramatic variation belongs—a variation which has had great positive effects, but also, as we have seen, many shabby and negative ones. He has therefore full right to be called the precursor of Wagner.

Besides the "Symphonie Fantastique," which undoubtedly blazed out a new path, Berlioz, stimulated by Byron's poem and Paganini's desire to have a piece composed by him for alto and orchestra, later on wrote another symphonic **work,** "Harold in Italy," which, in spite of its great beauties, cannot be said to reach the heights attained by his first symphony. Among his other works those which we have still to consider here are—besides the splendid overtures to the "Corsair," "King Lear," "Benvenuto Cellini," and the "Roman Carnival,"—the dramatic symphony "Romeo and Juliet," and the legendary "Damnation de Faust," which really enters into the realms of the opera.

In these two works, Berlioz, that musician of genius, shows himself in singular contrast to the rest of artistic humanity. Evidently his nature was attracted towards the opera; but the daring symphonist and orchestrator was not yet capable of that great advance which it was reserved for Richard Wagner to make, that is to say, of forming the music of his drama after the spirit of the poem, without disturbing his train of thought, an attempt to preserve the ancient operatic form.

Berlioz chose and arranged for himself operatic texts on old lines, then metamorphosized them by setting them to ravishingly beautiful pieces of music, which stand amongst the best we have in operatic music after the works of the old masters. Then he took the great dramas, already at that time very widely represented in France, such as Shakespeare's "Romeo and Juliet," and Goethe's "Faust," and appropriated them to his end.

This end was: to find, at any cost, the opportunity to pour out from his soul all the music, overflowing and violently compressed, which it contained; to produce music, and still more music, the most beautiful, the happiest that he was capable of creating. He did not even stop to examine if the form which he chose were artistically authorised. In reality it was not, as little in Berlioz as in Schumann's "Paradise and the Peri." It is rather a formless mixture of different modes of expression and styles, not entirely either oratorio, opera, or symphony: fragments of all, and consequently none of them complete.

In "Romeo and Juliet," a fugue paints the

104

fight between the hostile families; a long orchestral recitative tells of the intervention, remonstrance, and threat of the prince; short choral and solo passages tell of the unhappy fate of the lovers, of the power of love, and of the Fairy Queen Mab; big orchestral movements paint the ball at the house of Capulet, the love scene, and the fairy revels. This last tiny episode, so unimportant in the drama, returns twice, and, in consequence, the tragic conflict is totally neglected. A choral phrase expresses the grief of the women at the supposed death of Juliet; an orchestral passage, with voice, describes the awakening and tragic end of the lovers, and a finale, in correct operatic style, tells of the gathering of the people, the preaching of Father Lorenzo, and the reconciliation of the hostile parties. Berlioz chose the situations which seemed to him to be the most appropriate to his composition, without taking into account the organic enchantment of the whole.

In the "Damnation of Faust," he carried the commencement into Hungary. Why? Because, during a journey in Austria, after hearing the Rakocsy March he had brilliantly orchestrated it, and wished to make it known by putting it, as a component part, into some great work. So, originally enough, he created his own opportunity in making the play begin in Hungary; at least, this is what he himself confesses in the preface to the work. In order to have a reason for writing "A Descent into Hell" he made Faust descend into the infernal regions, contrary to the case in Goethe's poem, in which he is transfigured. Nevertheless Berlioz often makes use of the poem. This "Descent of Faust into Hell" is so congenial a movement that one scarcely regrets that he has violated the original poem of Goethe. And it is to the heresy, if I dare call it so, of having

106

turned the Queen Mab incident in "Romeo and Juliet" into a principal incident, that we are indebted for that marvellous scherzo, which is absolutely unique of its kind. In these two works, the other symphonic pieces are veritable marvels of fresh, spontaneous music, with the exception of one, of which I shall speak later. I may specially mention the brilliant "Fête at Capulet's," the beautiful and ardent love scene, and then, in the "Damnation of Faust," the dance of the Fairies and the Sylphs. I consider this work, above all, as being the most important of his creations after the "Symphonie Fantastique."

The psychological dramatic variation of a theme is employed in none of these later works, not even in the "Harold" symphony, with the same intensity as in the "Symphonie Fantastique." Berlioz had a grand idea, which he did not use himself, but of which the importance and fertility remain for the benefit of his successors. But supposing that all the productions of Berlioz do not seem to us to be perfect in form, in the highest and broadest sense of the word—even the works of which we last spoke—they have had, at least, a powerful influence on our artistic development. Berlioz has the right to be styled the Father of the new Modern School which is in force to-day, and whose representatives are generally in the greatest haste to attain new heights and achieve the strongest possible results. His work will show, throughout the whole development of the art of music, how this new school will always be capable of further advancement. He was not fortunate enough to possess that moral profundity, that ideal purity which causes the figure of Beethoven to stand out in such unspeakable grandeur. Nevertheless, after Beethoven, no composer except Wagner, has found so many new modes of musical expression, so many new lines of musical thought, as the great French musician. His boundless imagination will seem the more powerful, the richer, the more we search into his compositions, if we do but make of our study a veritable work of love. Like Schumann, Berlioz behaved very badly towards Wagner. In both cases we see the incapacity, or dislike, of one great man to acknowledge a greater, and this fact, unfortunately not rare, awakes in us a feeling anything but pleasant, for it reminds us that even highly gifted natures succumb to petty weaknesses of the spirit, and that the most enlightened minds are sometimes tortured by the tiny needles of jealousy when in sight of another's superiority. Let him who feels rising in himself such sentiments, and believes it out of his power to overcome them, turn towards that sublime example, which, in this respect, towers over all modern musicians; let him regard the venerable figure of Franz Liszt. This man,

himself so great, never ceased to make himself
of use to those artistic natures which were congenial to him; he undertook to make a
reputation for their works, assisted youthful
talent and genius in all branches; he ever
upheld them and sustained them with his
advice and his acts. Besides that, he never
undertook anything which would bring profit
to himself, and, too kind to others, he neglected
almost completely to take care of his own
creations. All this has been for many years
past a matter of history, and I am sure
that no one, even among those who do
not appreciate Liszt's compositions, would
wish to take from him the brilliant crown
which disinterestedness and the noblest charity
have placed upon his brow. In all that
concerns generosity, Liszt was the King of
Artists.

As a composer he surpasses Berlioz, in that
he preserves in his symphonic poems the old

form in a clear enough manner, side by side with an entire freedom of imagination. Berlioz generally wrote his movements gliding from one into the other, whereas Liszt keeps entirely away from that form, and so often gives to his work the character of an improvisation. His music is the direct issue of the poetic subject, of the fixed programme, and follows that programme alone in the musical expression to be given to the work. Sometimes he goes so far as to express in pieces and phrases of music, isolated thoughts and conditions of mind, placing them one against the other in the order prescribed in the programme.

Without any doubt, Liszt was, in this very procedure, preceded once by Berlioz in the penultimate movement of "Romeo and Juliet," which I have already mentioned. This movement is called "Romeo at the Tomb of Capulet; appeal to, and awakening of Juliet; ecstacy and first effects of poison; mental anguish and

death of the lovers." Berlioz tried here to
express the different points in the dramatic
action by melodic passages, phrasing, harmonic
combinations, or expressive ornamentation; he
essayed thus to represent them clearly enough
for the listener to understand the meaning of
each musical phrase as it was played. This
movement is given the least of any; for however well it is rendered, the impression it produces is absolutely foggy and indistinct, and
—my veneration for Berlioz does not prevent
me from saying—in certain places even ridiculous. The reason of this is that here he
required of music a task which she could not
accomplish.

If the title did not indicate to us the meaning
of the drama we should not, generally, know
what it was we heard, and we should have an
impression of a collection of sounds without
any definite sense. Naturally, we do not have
this impression when we know what the music

is supposed to represent, but, still, we are astonished to see how here the mere wording of the title is precise and clear compared to the music, which, under different circumstances, would give even a far more powerful impression than a great poem, well recited. We feel the same way at the commencement of "Romeo and Juliet," in the grand orchestral recitative, which is meant to represent the intervention of the Prince.

Only here this torturing impression soon passes off. Here we come to the point where the character of music makes itself manifest in all its majesty; here we see that it is an art which can never speak to us in abstractions, because, beyond the limit of abstract phrases, it shows the profoundest and truest traits of earthly existence in the most subtle pictures, and therefore stands far ahead of all her sister arts.

It is evident, then, that the grandeur of

music is impaired when the artist tries, as it
in so many words, to make it represent to our
minds actual occurrences, and that it is degraded and robbed of the peculiar tenderness
of its nature when it is explained measure by
measure, episode by episode, in a fixed programme. Music can express the feeling, the
sentiment, which an event engenders in the
soul, but it cannot picture the event itself.*
That is the task of poetry, and in one way
of the graphic and plastic arts; when notwith-
standing all this, music does undertake a like
impossible task, we feel a sensation similar
to that which we experience when, listening
to a person speaking in a language unknown
to us, we not only do not understand it, but
it seems even humorous and ridiculous to us.

* I here energetically refer to the only beautiful explanation of the essence of music in the two volumes
of Schopenhauer's "The World as Will and Idea."
The musician should not attach too much importance
to details, the total impression will never, according
to my idea, be secondary to it in value.

In such cases, as we have said, music is made to express sentiments which are out of its realm : it ceases then to be music. An imaginative mind cannot prevent itself from forming a mental picture on hearing a piece of music; that does not do any harm to the faculty of the comprehension, for beautiful music is raised on a pedestal more solid and trustworthy than the subject of that picture, and speaks to us with far greater power, no matter what it is. It tells us things of prodigious depth, by the side of which an event is only an image, an apparition. It unveils to us its secret, and renders it transparent (from which arises the extreme importance of music in the drama).

But, on the other hand, to take as a subject some event, either material or spiritual, dramatic or metaphysical, and try, through the medium of music, to express it in a series of adventures, otherwise, perhaps, than as a general expression of the life of the soul, is a foolish, nay, mad enterprise; for the word alone (even that in certain cases requires pictorial and plastic aid) possesses the power of such detailed expression. The artist is mistaken in the vehicle he employs. Another reason why it is an undertaking to be severely condemned is that it is the debasing of a sublime and noble art to a service far below its merits. Music, from being the original language of the Deity, has descended to a common, everyday mode of expression, and if ever the people become used to works of this kind, there will result a corruption of the musical faculty which would destroy all possibility of true masterpieces being understood. I have too firm a faith in the all-conquering force of music to believe in any real, lasting result from this tendency along new lines, from which faith springs my often criticised opposition to this sort of " fashionable nonsense."

Although the orchestral part of "Romeo and Juliet" served in some slight degree as a model for Liszt, he has composed works of infinitely greater value. In many of his compositions he used a form, which, while making the music describe the chosen programme, does not bind it to it, and is never foreign to the nature of music. But in each of these cases the form found by Liszt could only be used for expressing the particular poetic subject taken : for any other programme it would be absurd. Look at "Mazeppa," for instance, one of Liszt's most remarkable creations. A wildness, increasing to a mad fury, paints the "Ride to Death of the Hero"; a short andante expresses his prostration; the march which comes after growing into a song of supreme triumph, accompanied by trumpet blasts, paints his promotion and coronation.

Now let us pass to the symphonic poem "Orpheus," of which the form is but one great

117

crescendo and diminuendo: Orpheus touches the strings of his lute; worshipful, all nature listens to the marvellous sounds. With a noble step the god passes near to us, entrancing all by the glory of his person and his melodious voice. The tones of his lyre become more and more feeble, as we see the celestial form fading away in the distance, until finally it disappears entirely from our sight.* This arrangement, this increase from the softest pianissimo to the utmost plenitude of sound, is entirely authorised in itself and by its connection with the programme; but a piece constructed in a like manner, bearing the title of "Mazeppa," or a composition such as "Mazeppa" bearing the name "Orpheus," would be altogether impossible.

On the other hand, I am sure that if you should hear these poems without knowing their

---

* The form of the "Orpheus" poem is not unlike the "Lohengrin" overture.

names, you would recognise and feel in "Mazeppa" an element of tragic tempest, calming down, then rising again victorious; in "Orpheus," a being appearing and vanishing with the calmness of divine grandeur, without, in either case, knowing that the subjects were precisely Mazeppa and Orpheus. The mind is fixed on some special picture by the title, but without it the abstract intention would be perceived. The main thing will always be the general impression, not the meaning of this or that bar; above all, the work must possess a positive musical force, and not owe its original idea and invention to an inward craving for sensational picturing.

I consider it my duty to take up the defence of this kind of programme music, whilst condemning as severely as is in my power that other kind—a formless improvisation founded on uneventful abstractions. When, for instance, Liszt in his poem, "Les Ideales," tried

119

musically to interpret fragments of Schiller's poem in their order, and then to weld them together in one whole; when he goes so far, even, as to write at the head of each fragment the part of the poem which the music is intended to represent, so that, to tell the truth, only he who is provided with a score is able to know at each precise moment what he must conjure up, and he who has only the poem itself is absolutely at a loss to know where the music and the poem are connected; when a composer goes thus far, I say that the music must fall from on high, as would a bird deprived of a wing. Such is the case in "Les Ideales"; it cannot develop freely in accordance with its nature, for it is bound, from the beginning, to the successive fragments of the poem; that is to say, it is bound to a series of abstract ideas.

Compare it with the overture to the first version of "Fidelio," which is, properly speak-

ROBERT SCHUMANN.

ing, the "Leonora I" overture (generally and wrongly called the "Leonora II"). It is of less intrinsic value than the big one, but it is a correct operatic overture, for there are to be found in it all the separate events of importance in the drama which is to follow, such as the imprisonment of Florestan, the courageous efforts of Leonora to free her husband, her searching and enquiries, her meeting and fight with Pizzaro, the victory, a retrospective glance at their terrible experiences, amidst feelings of grateful recognition to God, and, finally, their infinite joy at being once more united. But how well Beethoven has understood how, besides expressing the dramatic action, to observe and keep intact the symphonic character of the music. And with what truly musical means he expresses the events! I remember the sudden powerful entry in C minor, instead of the ordinary reprisal of the first portion in C major: it represents the moment of greatest danger, the meeting of Leonora with Pizzaro. How unmistakably reminiscences of the opera, such as the passage where Pizzaro falls before Leonora's pistol, are brought to mind; and always without any violent shock.

I would hold up precisely this overture as a model, showing to what point a programme can be united to music, without doing damage to the latter's nature. From such poetic scenes were born the "Fingals' Cave" overture, by Mendelssohn, Schumann's "Manfred" overture, and the "Apotheosis of Sound" symphony by Spohr. The tendency to express musically these pictures and events even brought about, for a time, the junction of the two opposing schools.

At the beginning, as we can see by comparing Schumann with Liszt and Berlioz, it is not even altogether clear wherein lay the characteristics of the two different schools. Only at the coming of that completely abstract musician, Brahms, and at the appearance of the all dominating Wagner, did one begin to see clearly two oppositely opposed styles. When the power of Wagner began to make itself felt, the disciples of the classics saw how untenable was become their position, and played Brahms as a trump card. The directions were clearly defined.

To-day there are so many composers that everybody feels obliged to agitate in the interests of some particular one. Those, however, who do not belong to any party, give general offence by their compositions, and can only trust the sound feeling of the people, who in spite of erroneous doctrines, always find the truth at last, though, only, perhaps, after a long while.

Here, I should like to issue a warning against a capital mistake, which I have found in very many recent compositions : that is a mixture of

123

the dramatic and symphonic styles. Whilst re-
calling to mind what Wagner has written on
the subject in his "Use of Music in the
Drama," this is what I should add: except
in a few isolated cases a characteristic feature
of symphony subjects should be their breadth,
and their essentially melodic character, whereas
the musico-dramatic theme should distinguish
itself by its relief and its significant concise-
ness. A symphonic movement could never be
constructed out of one of Wagner's themes,
even the most harmonically simple. Nor could
the first subject of the "Eroïca" (which, by
the way, is composed of twelve bars, not of
four, as many people believe), the melodies of
Beethoven's slow movements, nor any symphony themes in general, be employed in the
formation of an opera.

The sentiment which inspires the inventive
faculty of a dramatist, is altogether different
from that which affects the symphonist. Real

living people, representing actual events on the stage, to the dramatist, suggest motives, plastic and full of meaning, which often unveil to our eyes, even more clearly than words could do, the full importance of those events. The symphonist, on the other hand, is inspired to compose by spiritual feelings more deeply placed, by a contemplative nature, by the greatest and noblest stirrings of the mind, by events which, whether true or imaginary, have no need of dramatic impersonation.

The work of the symphonist should be, to a certain extent, the revelation of his own soul in the language of sound, thus causing the necessity for a grandeur of theme and of melodic instrumentation which in the drama is rarely possible.

If we can use the word "symphony" in connection with an orchestral passage in a musical drama when constructed with acknowledged meaning, in the polyphonic style of the drama, we can also call a symphony "dramatic" if the fundamental basis of the work be passionate and varied in sentiment. The world is one great drama, of which music reveals to us the most hidden thoughts; in this sense, music itself is "dramatic," as we can see in the works of our great master, Beethoven, to whose figure we must continually return in order to understand thoroughly each other on the subject. So let us introduce the word "symphonic" in its concrete meaning into the musical drama, and the word "dramatic" in its metaphysical sense into the symphony movement; only let us beware of the consequent confusion, which would give birth to music more closely allied to operatic fragments than to the symphony.

Decidedly worthy of notice, but to-day not sufficiently noted or heeded, is the way in which Wagner makes understood the necessity for severely keeping to one tonality, so long as there is no manifest reason for quitting it. He explains that this necessity exists even more in the symphony than in the drama, because the daring harmonic progressions which, in the latter, result directly from the scenic action would, in the former, be absolutely incomprehensible.

There are few requirements against which so many sins are committed to-day as against this, which was the flesh and blood of all the great masters, including Wagner. The greater number of Brückner's symphonies, for instance, suffer from this incessant and stupid modulation; it is sometimes difficult to see why one is said to be in E major, and another in C minor, when often it is only the last two bars which indicate the key of the movement, the intermediate parts wandering like lost sheep through all the tonalities.

But, on the other hand, Wagner does not appear to me to be right, when he objects to the transformation of a theme such as is necessary in the drama (the psychologico-dramatic variation—to use my own term) as being in the symphony an *effet cherché*. Although only in a slight degree, the sudden entry of the minor, which I have already spoken of in the first "Leonora" overture, is already a closely resembling variation of the same theme appearing earlier in the major. Later, when in Liszt's "Mazeppa," the fearfully increasing rapidity of the ride to death is expressed by a continual shortening of the rhythm, by a breathless shortening of the principal theme from $\frac{6}{4}$ to $\frac{4}{4}$ time, and from $\frac{3}{4}$ to $\frac{2}{4}$; when, further on still, the principal subject makes itself heard at the end of the march in conquering triumph, those variations do not have the effect of being at all unnatural, but rather of being absolutely spontaneous, and, being in the character of the music, show the power of musical expression.

As in the drama these variations are bound by the action, so in the symphony they should submit themselves to the laws of symphonic form, whether it be the old or the new style that the musician, led away by his subject, has chosen. In truth, if anyone were to question me about the rule of such new form, I should have to reply with Hans Sachs, "It imposes itself on, and follows after you."

Yes, that following on, that continuous, inexorable enforcing of the self-imposed rule; that non-deviation, from which results the clearness of a work; that labour by the sweat of the brow, if necessary, until little by little inspiration springs forth, leaving no traces of any kind that the apparent spontaneity is the result of hard work and trouble—that is what constitutes a real work of art. There is no benefit to be obtained from leaving the old form without some definite reason; it is absurd to call the upholding of the form "reaction." The modern Germans, the reactionaries, forget that by their fury against the existing form they become as prejudiced and wrong as the so-called classicists in their disbelief in the possibility of an innovation.

All depends upon what the work has to tell us as a whole: the form will always be only the complete adequate expression of the contents. Naturally, this only concerns masterpieces, not futile attempts by every bungler who thinks he can hide his ignorance behind a pathetic programme, and then wants to make us believe afterwards that he meant the work to appear thus limping in a scattered and broken way.

Some of the other works by Liszt suffer from the same faults as "Les Ideales"; for instance, "Hamlet," "Prometheus," and "Heroide Funèbre," which are also inferior through a certain lack of force in inspiration. A sort of improvisation, as though the work were made up bit by bit, is peculiar to the compositions of Liszt. One might say that, as in Brahms, the dominating feature is an element of dreamy reflection, which in Liszt becomes rhapsodic, and in his poorer compositions, and also in the "Mountain Symphony," otherwise so rich in beautiful details, becomes very noticeable and annoying. Besides those just mentioned; "Mazeppa" and "Orpheus," "Hungaria," "Festklänge," "The Battle of the Huns"—a fantastic piece of elementary, dismal power, "Les Preludes," the ideally beautiful "Tasso," and, above all, the two great symphonies to "Faust" and Dante's "Divine Comedy" are masterpieces in which this rhapsodic form reaches the apogee of its force and power of expression.

The "Faust Symphony" is not, perhaps, intended actually to describe musically Goethe's poem, but it gives, as the title will tell, the drawings of the three characters,

Faust, Gretchen and Mephistopheles. The third movement shows us with what skill and imagination Liszt made use of the "leit-motiv" idea, similar to that of which I showed Berlioz to be the originator. Mephistopheles is "Der Geist der Stets verneint," for all that is born is worthy to perish : that is the basis of his influence. So Liszt did not give him a theme of his own. He built up the whole movement by caricaturing the preceding ones —principally the Faust motive—which has been the cause of absurd statements that he was lacking in faculty of invention, even more so than in the case of Berlioz. I ask you this : if the old masters created great move-ments on motives only a few bars in length, on which they made different variations, should not the same thing be permitted to a musician inspired by a recognisable poetic idea? Does not this very variation require an inventive power?

132

And precisely this movement of the "Faust" symphony shows us—nothing could do so better—how profound was Liszt's knowledge of the true nature of music. When the power of the fiend has attained its full force, the principal theme of the Gretchen movement makes its appearance in all its primitive beauty, floating, as it were, in radiant clouds. At the contact, the spell is broken, and falls back into nothingness. The poet left Gretchen in the depths of shame, in order to represent her as a criminal: the musician, according to the ideal and subtle character of his art, leaves us with an impression of her at once sublime and full of light.

Powerful trumpet blasts resound through the expiring infernal music; a male chorus begins to sing softly the sublime words of Goethe's mystic choir, "Alles Vergängliche ist nur ein Gleichniss"; then, in the easily recognised tones of the Gretchen motive, a tenor voice continues: "Das Ewig-Weibliche zieht uns hinan." It is easy to identify this tenor voice with Goethe's Doctor Marianus, to imagine to oneself the transfiguration of Gretchen by the side of the Mater Gloriosa. The words of Faust when he sees the disappearing image of Gretchen, are also called to mind:

> " And like unto the beauty of the soul,
>   Her lovely form arises, nor dissolves,
>   But floating upwards, t'wards the ethereal blue,
>   It steals the best our inmost soul contains."

So, in great works, do threads of gold weave themselves between the music and the poetry that inspires it: light, floating sunbeams, which embellish both arts without binding either of them.

Of a still greater unity, and perhaps still more powerful than the "Faust" symphony, is the music to Dante's "Divine Comedy," with its expressive picture of the infernal tortures and Purgatory, rising higher and higher, towards the utmost heights of purity of sentiment.*

To these two works Liszt gave all the best his nature contained. They mark the zenith of his creative power, and, excepting those of Berlioz, they are the most perfect examples of truly artistic programme music which exist.

It is gratifying and satisfactory to observe that the creations of Liszt and Berlioz are ever gaining more and more ground and comprehension, and now even arouse enthusiasm, although a great many critics take the opportunity of nagging at them, or abusing them with their traditional superiority, whenever they are played.

The pseudo-classics turn up their noses, and

---

* At the request of the ultra-catholic Princess Wittgenstein, Liszt composed a second ending, illustrating the Church triumphant: but it is very feeble. I advise its absolute extermination.

135

the ultra-modern would willing consider these two masters as already-passed landmarks to perfection, where "New gods are now enthroned." Their hopes are vain.

Time gives its powerful verdict without paying attention to the pigmies puffing themselves up, and crawling about in narrow-minded nullity; and already one begins to understand that Berlioz and Liszt were, with Wagner, the great stars of the new epoch of music, the heroes of the second part of the nineteenth century, in the same way as Haydn, Mozart, Beethoven, Weber and Schubert were those of the first.

Excepting these two symphonies of several movements, Liszt's orchestral works are generally composed of one single one, and are called "symphonic poems."

The denomination is good, and appears to me to contain, in two words, the rule, the only one, perhaps, which should be imposed on a

From a photo by Reutlinger, Paris.

HECTOR BERLIOZ.

piece of music in order that it may have the right to exist. Let it be a "poem"; that is to say, let it owe its conception to a poetic idea, to an impulse of the soul, which will either remain unexpressed, or be made known to the public by means of a title and programme; but let it be also symphonic or, in other words, musical. It must also have a form, either classic or modern, derived from the subject, or conforming to it in spirit. In art the absence of form is always reprehensible, and in music can never be excused, either by a programme or by what the composer imagined to himself. Just as a big boulder, in which one sees a suggestion of a human face and limbs, can never be called a statue, so it is impossible to call a formless collection of sounds, arising from some vague idea, a piece of music. Liszt's symphonic works mark a great first step on the new road. He who would wish to advance further upon it must

137

aim, above all, not to imitate a method of writing piece by piece, often enough, remarkable with this composer, but to write compositions which will be more than mere illustrations of programmes.

I hope to have shown clearly enough, how the modern school, of which Liszt and Berlioz are the most important representatives, has brought forth both good and bad results. It has shown us that there are other available forms than the inevitable sonata, rondo, and "theme and variation," thus opening to the imagination a dangerous field of possibilities, it is true, but in which much good fruit can still be gathered. But, on the other hand, it has to a certain extent degraded music from its ancient and venerable degree to being the humble slave of the word and the conception. It is often a difficult, always a delicate matter to recognise the boundary beyond which music must not go, if it is not to become anti-musical: in order that that frontier be clearly defined, a large number of new and important works are doubtless necessary.

Let the younger generation of composers be and remain persuaded that music is not an abstract language. Let it recognise that *form* is indispensable, and know how to distinguish the symphonic from the dramatic style. Then we may hope for some composer, who, knowing all this, will give us symphonies which will really tell us something, and not be mere problems set up to be resolved.

CHAPTER IV.

WE gather from all this that the modern school has been far more fruitful in results than the neo-classic. It has become the leaven in the bread in the house of the Philistines, and the rising becomes more noticeable every day in Germany as well as in other countries.

I firmly believe that many really worthy modern symphonies would not be what they are, if Liszt and Berlioz had not lived.

Amongst others I might mention those of Sinding and Borodin.

Again, we see nowadays many passages in

the old style in works of the modern school, a desertion to the enemy's camp, as it were. Already becoming old, Dvorák, who might be called a pupil of Brahms, and has obtained much success with his symphonies, has suddenly turned his face towards programme music, and composes symphonic poems.

We saw, several years ago, a similar conversion of Richard Strauss, who is still quite young.

As a pupil of Hans von Bülow, who had abandoned the Wagner faction, he swore fidelity to Brahms, and wrote an excellent symphony of model form. Later he became a modern of moderns, and has composed a series of symphonic poems, of which we must not, for a long time yet, expect to see the last.

I consider as his greatest work, and far superior to "Don Juan," which, however, is better known and preferred, the wonderfully powerful "Death and Transfiguration," a piece full of originality, admirably constructed, and inspired by a truly pure and sincere sentiment as far as the finale, which seems to me to represent pomposity, rather than transfiguration.

I hold to be of equal value the orchestral scherzo entitled "The merry pranks of Till Eulenspiegel," with its brilliant themes and orchestration, and, if the term be allowed in a musical sense, its extreme wittiness.

In "Thus Spake Zarathustra," Strauss falls into the same mistakes as Liszt in "Les Ideales." Just as Liszt wished in that work to paint a series of events which elevate humanity to a higher existence, so Strauss causes to pass before us a series of terrestrial views, of which each one endeavours to solve the Eternal Puzzle by the melodic progression C G C! Not one succeeds, and at the end the C G C are still there, just as obstinate as at the beginning; the meaning is still clouded over

142

by that doubt, which, according to Nietzsche, is "the Father of Truth," and to Strauss the chord C E F sharp.

Admitting the possibility of musically expressing isolated feelings, such as those of religion, of joy and sorrow, of superhuman Bacchanalian gaiety—such as in the last movement of Beethoven's A major Symphony—and that it is feasible to symbolise by a fugue the powerlessness of science to solve the last and highest question, nevertheless, through the compression of so many different sentiments into one movement, and consequently the further necessity of the hearer to unravel the web of indubitably rich ideas, the impression of music, in the true sense of the word, is lost.

Besides these faults, which even the most masterly handling of the orchestra is not able to disperse, it seems to me also as if the positive force of invention in this composition were

inferior to that in the earlier compositions of
Strauss; for which I can find no good reason,
except that the way from inspiration to execution has passed the empire of abstraction, and
that the music thus attempts to invade a
domain which is, and always will remain, inaccessible to it; it seems therefore, to be always
seeking the right way, without finding it, and
to be losing its strength in experimental wan-
derings. Quite as much as in "Zarathustra,"
Strauss in his newest works, "Don Quixote"
and "A Hero's Life," breaks away from what
I understand by the word music. With the
old masters we can do without a programme;
with Berlioz and Liszt the title is generally
sufficient. Strauss considers it necessary,
before the appearance of a new work, to send
out detailed explanations and textbooks,
written by other persons. Why does he need
these, when he actually believes in his unlim-
ited power of giving such a distinctness of

From a photo by A. Meyer, Berlin.

RICHARD STRAUSS.

meaning to his music that it is able to speak to us at once, as though in words? If he could do that, we would listen to what he had to say to us, without explanation, and without programme. Then his task would have been fulfilled.

On the occasion of the first representation of "Till Eulenspiegel," certain as he was of the musical character of the piece, he had delicately—remembering some "Eulenspiegel" anecdotes, I might even say tactfully—refused programmes. Of the meaning of this piece, even if it had been given without a title, we would have a decided and clear impression, although we would by no means have needed to think specially of the "Eulenspiegel."

In his latter pieces it is different. Nobody, for instance, will see in the great violin solo in "Heldenleben," that it represents a woman holding herself aloof at first, but whose love the hero is by degrees winning; or in the dis-

cordant horn passage in the second part
think of the hero's adversary, if he does not
know that he is supposed to imagine these
things.

This way of influencing the public beforehand, which the author considers necessary,
proves, however, that the new way he pretends
to follow is only an apparently true one; these
detailed explanations being, in reality, nothing
but avowals that the work itself, with all its
artifices of polyphony, and with all the sur-
prises of instrumentation, contains, only misty
forms if those explanations are not given. On
the other hand, there is no real programme
joined to them, and the public is thus, so to
speak, only indirectly brought to comprehension, being told abstractly what it may think,
and then having to consider it all as explicit
speaking.

This imperfection, which, as we have already
remarked, characterises all these extravagant

compositions—the more noticeable in that they certainly possess originality as to clever harmonic combinations, although none with regard to melodies and themes—is entirely absent from natural, spontaneous compositions.

The truly new stands perfect, free and upright by itself, and steps boldly out into the world; it needs no preliminary explanation as a crutch.

There have been many æsthetic questions discussed with regard to Strauss's compositions; among others, it has been declared absurd to attempt to represent a flock of sheep, as in "Don Quixote," in a piece of music. According to my idea, it depends how it is done, and in what surroundings. A mere imitation of the natural sound, as Strauss has represented it, may, with skill, be made worthy of approbation, in the same way as, for instance, a painting which in a masterly realistic way represents a dung heap may show the

147

painter's splendid technical power. In both cases there is perfume wanting to make the illusion perfect. A really artistic representation in tones of a flock of bleating sheep would certainly have been less true, but more full of spirit, humour and music than is the case here.

If some of Strauss's compositions, in which, on the principle that as nothing is perfect everything is permissible, he piles ugliness on ugliness, induce us to believe that this composer—who from his early youth has been spoiled by acknowledgment and applause, and who, it may scarcely surprise you to know, takes himself as the hero in his latest works— has tried in a moment of foolishness to see to what degree the people would be gulled, thus indulging in buffoonery, much as Bülow did in his concert lectures, and very often, I think, in his conducting—it is, however, not the harmonious and instrumental abomination, but chiefly the above mentioned more important

148

objection which prevents us from approving of Strauss creations during the last few years. His brilliant, indeed, sensational success cannot lead me astray, and in general to those who elevate their minds above the apparitions of the day to the history of centuries a contemporary success must seem of very ephemeral value.

Here I wish to mention the singular experience which I have often had, but which I have never heard confirmed by others. When I hear a piece which shows up the weakness of modern programme music, after a short time of careful attention, I feel, in spite of the great outward difference, just as I do when I hear a feeble work by Brahms; exactly the same irritated, insipid, empty, morose feeling!

Does this similarity of effect spring from the fact that Brahms's music appears to me as an abstraction, contrary to its nature, whilst in pieces of programme music, abstractions, in contrast to actualities, are expressed? Will not the false, artificial and therefore anti-artistic branches of the two schools finally be as close to each other, as their great productions, which have incontestible similarity, would show? Looking at them from a distance, does there not seem to be only one instead of two schools? Only later on will it be possible to answer this question.

Since I spoke some time ago of an old man and a young one, permit me to apply the same comparison, otherwise purely external, to two other artists. Directly under the influence of Liszt, Frederick Smetana, the Bohemian, wrote a series of six symphonic poems. He gave them as general title, "My Fatherland," because he drew his inspiration from a Bohemian legend. I may mention particularly the "Vlatava" (Moldau), the "Vysehrad," and the "Forest and Plains of Bohemia," as possessing great merits.

150

The first mentioned work is a particularly good example of how far a descriptive programme is compatible with beautiful music. Another important figure in these days is that of Gustave Mahler, who is not nearly enough known in his capacity of composer. His works are colossal in structure, but demand the help of extraordinary numerous forces, which renders them difficult both to perform and listen to.

If we pass over these, in any case secondary objections, and turn to the composer himself, we recognise a deep and strong feeling, which both can and does express itself freely, and, careless of the possibility of execution and success, says exactly what it wishes to say. One characteristic of Mahler is the important length of his themes. He is a musician to the depth of his soul, and in many ways an artistic relative of his master Bruckner, only he knows better than did the latter how to work out his themes and build up the whole work. There are to be found in his works peculiarities and difficulties without apparent motive: one might almost say that there is too much spinning out; that the author in his choice of themes did not watch himself carefully enough. Nevertheless, all that Mahler has written bears the stamp of a rich imagination, and ardent, almost fanatical enthusiasm.

Now, having considered the modern men, especially the most modern, Strauss and Mahler, who are still living and at the zenith of their productions, let us look forward from the present into the future. Whether an artist will be given to us who will advance by his own originality the works of Berlioz, Liszt and Wagner, thus making himself worthy to be counted amongst the greatest men of genius we cannot yet tell.

It is not forbidden to us to imagine such a master, and to think of him as he would have

Photo by Bieber, Berlin.

GUSTAV MAHLER.

to be in our days. I see a man, above all, independent of all party feeling, mingling with none, because he overtops them all; he is neither shabbily German, nor weakly cosmopolitan, rather he imparts the sentiment of all humanity, for music is a universal art; he is imbued with an ardent, infinite enthusiasm for the creations of great geniuses of the past, of all time and all nationalities; he feels an insurmountable antipathy for mediocrity, with which he is only brought into contact by contrast.

He appears to me as being without jealousy, because conscious of the real value of his own works, and confident of them—disdaining even, to countenance any paltry propaganda of them. He is much disliked in many circles, because of his profound sincerity, and his contempt for public opinion. He does not anxiously pose for the world at large, but rather prefers solitude; he does not take a pessimistic view of life, but, being repulsed by the general meanness and pettiness of spirit, only chooses a few rare exceptions as his boon companions.

Nor does he appear to my imagination as insensible either to success, or the lack of it, only incapable of turning one step out of his set path for one or the other: in his political ideas, he is republican in the same sense as Beethoven.

I see him, as it were, walking in the Alpine regions of Switzerland, midst the clear, white, overtowering summits which, though familiar, still inspire veneration; I see him there, walking always with his eyes fixed on some very high peak, and advancing towards it with great strides. While feeling himself related only to the greatest geniuses, still he knows himself to be but a new link in the chain formed by them, and he feels that other great powers will come after him. Certainly he

154

belongs to a school, but a school which floats above the heads of humanity and keeps aloof from it.

Now, leaving this play of the imagination aside, we come back to realities, we must recognise that at the present moment there is a sort of interegnum of music, a veritable standstill. Everywhere, one feels a nervous, uneasy agitation, an aimless groping, with an obscure design, a race for success and celebrity, at all costs and by any means. "Progress," "New German School," "A Non-existent Originality," "Progone," "Epigone," "Eclectics," "Founder of a New School," "An End Overreached"; such are a few of the numerous, noisy expressions which resound in our ears. At one moment some one tells us of a new symphonic poem, in comparison with which the works of Wagner, Liszt and Berlioz are but Tom Thumbs; at another, of a composition in which can again be found the true national character. Like Will-o'-the-Wisps, new figures pass by us, grow dimmer, and disappear.

Into judgment and musical taste, is often instilled an almost frivolous delight in existing caprice, irregularities and deformities. Formerly, the Philistine used to cross himself at each tritone, and watched anxiously for each place where a crossing of the parts occurred; nowadays every harmonic impurity is called "boldness," especially if there is no motive, and those who advance still further in that direction are honoured by the title of "Reformer." Doubtless, in the midst of this confusion, the really great, the true, the original, silently grows in strength, far from the hum of the common market of art.

Its appearance will not only be a personal question, but a question of culture. The artist cannot keep distant from the rest of the world. He must gather his ideas, his inspirations and his standard from life itself. Is it possible that in this epoch of intense nervous and busy existence, in the midst of the commotion and continual rush, there will be found in any one soul enough contemplation and sincerity to bring forward a few works of art which would not be more or less basely stamped with the hall mark of their period? Will that grandeur without pathos, that grace without coquetry, that force and charm of the spirit which distinguish our great masters return, without any reaction, on the basis of the ideas we have accumulated up till to-day?

In this epoch of technique, inventions and commerce, is such a condition of art possible as, standing out far beyond its time, would still—like everything great—also be a child of it? This question, also, must be left to the future. We may, however, in the meantime gain the certain conviction that true progress does not come from without, but from within. If the artistic creation is merely speculative, and not impulsive, it may startle, but never warm us, nor will it ever be able to obtain immortality. Whoever agrees with me in what I have said, will join me in exhorting thus all young composers whose character can yet be moulded: Think and live in greatness as our great masters did: then your production will be true, and as it comes from your soul, so will it be good.

If you cannot do this, it is of no use to accumulate Ossa on Pelion; to write for a thousand trombones and two hundred thousand kettledrums: only a frightful noise will result. Brilliant skill alone is not sufficient. Simplicity, frank and robust sincerity, that is what we need. Write bravely what you feel in your soul, and express what should be given forth. Then it will be a likeness of yourself, a manifestation of your nature, and in every case complete and good.

Have also the courage to remain yourself,

158

even if misunderstood, and pulled to pieces. But do not think it is necessary to produce a work like the Ninth Symphony, or the Tetralogy. The world will be very grateful for an opera such as those of Lortzing, a symphony such as Hermann Goetz composed, if what you have produced is pure and natural.

Do not imagine you are a superior being, if the principles of Zoroaster fly around your ear misunderstood, and put your brain into a condition of unhealthy hallucination. It is only permitted to a few to wander in the high places of humanity, and the necessary superiority can neither be learnt nor made. It must come from another region, a very rare gift, a present of the greatest value. From what region? you ask curiously. Well, from one which can only be denied by those whose cheeks have never received a touch of its breath.

Whether you have composed a tiny "lied" or a great symphony, it will only be a true masterpiece if Beethoven's inscription on the manuscript score of the "Messe Solennelle" can be applied to it:

"This work comes from the heart: May it go back to it!"

INDEX

161

APPENDIX.

---

*SYMPHONY No. 5, IN C MINOR (WEINGARTNER).

By D. C. Parker.

FELIX WEINGARTNER'S fame as a conductor is so great that one is in danger of forgetting that he has a long list of works to his credit. He has just completed a new one, which had its first performance in Edinburgh on December 8, when it was played by the Scottish Orchestra, under the composer's direction. This symphony is the fifth which Weingartner has written, and it is in the key of C minor. The symphony is laid out in four movements, an opening allegro, a scherzo, an adagio, and a finale. The chief interest of his

---

* In "The Musical Standard," January 10, 1925.

165   13

most recent composition lies in the revelation of his artistic personality which it gives us. Weingartner is not one of those who look upon the past with contempt and speak of it with a cheap sneer. Whether he be in fashion, or out of it, is not likely to worry him. He knows perfectly well that for which he stands, as this symphony conclusively proves. The new work comes from an experienced, talented and sincere musician, whose outlook on music is sane and broad. Structurally, it does not depart from tradition. In listening to it one was, in fact, impressed by its orthodoxy. Only in the finale does the composer introduce us to something a little out of the common. This finale takes the form of a fugue with two themes. It is built up with immense skill and culminates in a cleverly devised fusion of the themes—a moment which proves to be the most arresting in the entire work.

Listening to the music one learned much of Weingartner's mentality. His symphony seems to tell us that he does not believe that melody is a thing to be despised. He is not ashamed to write a recognisable theme, and he is not ashamed to show his delight in doing so. The two subjects of the opening movement are well contrasted, the first being of a strong, dynamic nature and possessing horizontal interest. This theme has driving power, strength and vigour. A little tail-piece on the wood-winds, which comes at the end of it, is delightful, and haunts one after the performance is over. The second subject is of a lyrical nature, and soars high on the violins. When writing his scherzo the composer seemed determined to show that it was possible to do something while imposing upon himself an unusual simplicity. The light, tripping measure which opens this movement is very naïve, as is also the theme of the trio, which might almost have come from Haydn. The slow movement is the work of a romanticist, whose romanticism is held in check by his classical bias. Needless to say, one of the features of the new symphony lies in its artful scoring. Weingartner does not overload the page. Indeed, it is one of his merits that he does not call upon an instrument unless for some particular reason; but this wise economy is the economy of a man who has spent all his life in close touch with the orchestra, a man who knows every secret of it.

The symphony is pleasing rather than great. It does not sound the heroic note; it is not, perhaps, very profound; but it can be heard with pleasure, and it emanates from a man who does not believe that romance is dead, or that melody is a mark against a work. Of the four parts, the finale is undoubtedly the finest. The composer put before himself a very stiff proposition. It is not easy to interest an audience in a final movement which consists of a fugue with two themes, but it is a tribute to Weingartner's contrapuntal skill, his knowledge of effect, and his musicianly qualities generally, that this movement found so much favour with those who heard it. The significance of the work lies in this fact; it tells us that Weingartner is one who is willing to learn from the past, and who, while not uncritical in his attitude to it, sees no reason to cut himself off from what he feels to be of true worth.